"WE SERVE TO SAVE"

THE HISTORY
OF THE
MACK VOLUNTEER FIRE DEPARTMENT
TO THE
GREEN TOWNSHIP FIRE & EMS

Joe Flickinger

HERITAGE BOOKS
2023

HERITAGE BOOKS

AN IMPRINT OF HERITAGE BOOKS, INC.

Books, CDs, and more—Worldwide

For our listing of thousands of titles see our website
at
www.HeritageBooks.com

Published 2023 by
HERITAGE BOOKS, INC.
Publishing Division
5810 Ruatan Street
Berwyn Heights, MD 20740

Heritage Books by the author:

A Bicentennial History of Green Township: Uncovering a Jewel in the Crown of the Queen City, 1809–2009

A History of Bridgetown Cemetery: Quietly Serving Cincinnati's Western Hills for over 150 Years

A History of Colerain Township: From Frontier Wilderness to Suburban Sprawl

"We Serve to Save": The History of the Mack Volunteer Fire Department to the Green Township Fire & EMS

International Standard Book Number
Paperbound: 978-0-7884-2980-4

Dedication

This book is written as a tribute to the men and women who dedicated their lives to keeping the citizens of Green Township safe.

Table of Contents

List of Illustrations

Foreword

The Mack Volunteer Fire Department was established in 1944 to provide emergency fire and medical services to the citizens of Green Township, Hamilton County, Ohio. Over the years, this department endured many challenges and changes, and today *remains* one of the most progressive departments in Western Hamilton County, under the name of Green Township Fire & EMS. Those left from the volunteer era created a non-profit/charitable organization known as Mack Fire Incorporated, which provides a financial donation annually.

In 2018, a current member of Green Township Fire & EMS (and former Mack Fire Department Volunteer) suggested the creation of a "history book" to capture a glimpse into the first 75 years of this organization. With the help of several members procuring old artifacts, along with first-hand experiences, Joe Flickinger graciously designed and produced *"We Serve to Save": The History of the Mack Volunteer Fire Department to the Green Township Fire & EMS.*

Flickinger, a Green Township resident, has years of history-related experience as an accomplished writer, author, high school history teacher, and member of the Green Township Historical Association. His patience and diligent work ethic allowed the dream for a fire department history book to come to fruition. Thank you Joe for a quality project, that undoubtedly would not have occurred without your talents, persistence, and leadership. We are forever grateful!

Scott G. Souders
Chief of Department
Green Township Fire & EMS

Acknowledgments

I want to thank the members of Mack Fire Inc and Chief Scott Souders of the Green Township Fire & EMS for giving me their trust to write the history of the fire service in Green Township. I would especially like to thank Dwight Waldorf and his colleagues on the committee from Mack Fire Inc for their assistance with accessing the archives of Mack Fire Inc. Their diligence in organizing and preserving the items from the beginnings of the Mack Volunteer Fire Department has allowed for this book to be written. Thank you to everyone who passed along pictures, stories, and anecdotes. To my former students in my Cincinnati History class, who encouraged me to write books on local history- without your encouragement, I would have never dreamt that I could add to the historical record. To my parents, Bill and Nancy Flickinger, who instilled their love of history in me and passed on to me the respect and admiration I have for the local fire department. I hope this book continues to make you proud. I would also like to thank Paul Ruffing, Julie Carpenter, and Fred Matson for their editorial assistance. Finally, to my wife Kathleen, and my children Erin, Ryan, and Kelsey, thank you for putting up with my unending fascination and interest in local history.

Introduction

"Call the guys from Mack!" Many residents of Green Township repeated this line many times from 1944 to 1983 during emergencies. From 1983 to now, Green Township Fire & EMS has answered the same call. One thing that has not changed is the dedication both organizations have provided to the people of Green Township. Whether it is major structural fires, auto accidents, medical events, school visits, or everything in between, these men and women have been there for the citizens of Green Township. The Mack Volunteer Fire Department was established in 1944 due to a lack of fire and emergency medical care in Green Township. This organization contracted with Green Township for protection services in under-protected township areas. The service areas grew as time passed, and new firehouses were constructed to keep up with demand as the township population swelled in the 1970s due to the baby boom. By the mid-1980s, the volunteer department began to transfer services to the Green Township government. The Green Township-Mack Fire Department was formed. This fire and EMS service continued the tradition started by the Mack Volunteer. This department was recently renamed Green Township Fire & EMS and has continued the tradition of protecting the lives and property of the citizens of Green Township under the auspices of the township government. The story of these departments is one of dedication, service, and loyalty to the people of Green Township. They put their lives on the line by running into buildings that people run out of and risk injury when an auto accident on a roadway has someone trapped in a precarious position. The story of these two organizations, both pillars of the community, will instill a sense of pride in the people and property they have saved over the years. This book examines the growth and evolution of these two departments through their service to the community. Without these men and women dedicating themselves to protecting the people of Green Township, many citizens would have undoubtedly died or suffered significant personal loss. This book details the emergence of these organizations and their trials and tribulations. I hope this book finds you swelling with pride as you read about the brave history of the men and women who protected and continue to protect Green Township.

Chapter One:
Green Township's Early History and Firefighting Efforts

The Mack Volunteer Fire Department was in Mack, an unincorporated community in the Cincinnati suburb of Green Township, Hamilton County, Ohio. Inhabitants of Green Township and its encompassing communities are very familiar with the area, but many native Cincinnatians are unfamiliar with the western side of Cincinnati. As native Cincinnatians know it, Green Township can be a puzzle to many "outsiders" because of its unique closeness and small-town feel within ten miles of a major Midwestern city. Many outsiders venture into Green Township to visit friends and relatives or attend community events and emerge surprised and bewildered by the unique names of streets, neighborhoods, and community institutions. The Green Township of today bears little resemblance to the Green Township of pioneer days when Native Americans considered this area their "sacred hunting ground."[1] The Green Township of pioneer days was frontier land, far removed from the small settlement known to many as Losantiville (Cincinnati today). The area was dotted with beautiful trickling streams with many types of fish and lands filled with other wildlife such as deer, rabbit, and the occasional bear. This land of the late 1700s also had lush, thick forests, making travel through the area by wagon almost impossible unless travelers followed Native American trails. Travel on foot or horseback was an absolute necessity, as many of these trails were less than five feet wide, making settlement in the area very slow.

---

[1] Hale, Harry J, "Kuliga, The Pretty Land; The colorful story of Green Township , Hamilton County Ohio." Western Hills Press. 1949, 3

To understand the settlement patterns of Green Township, one must follow many of the obstacles in the way of the area's early settlers. The Native Americans in the area, the Shawnee, were very hostile towards American settlement in the land north of the Ohio River as they considered the Ohio Country as their "sacred hunting ground." At first, many American hunters and trappers navigated through the area and made positive contact with the Shawnee and other tribes living in the Ohio Country.

These hunters and trappers hunted for a few months, bartered and traded with the local tribes, and moved on quickly. This contact occurred until the end of the American Revolution when the Proclamation of 1763 was repealed; the settlement opened to just about anyone who wished to move to the newly opened "wild west." The Proclamation of 1763 forbade further settlement into the Ohio territory by British subjects. However, this treaty did not stop some of the settlers. Making a fresh start lured individuals to this new territory, creating a new beginning where they could substantially change their lives. Despite the Proclamation of 1763, settlement increased, with many individuals choosing the Ohio Valley as an excellent place to start a new life. Many of these settlers were native Virginians; by settling in the Ohio Valley, they chose to stay Virginians because Virginia had claimed a large chunk of the territory. Many Virginians who moved here believed that the British Royal agents who oversaw Virginia would ignore the movement in violation of the Proclamation. This inattention was mainly due to the significant distance between the main urban areas of eastern Virginia and the Ohio territory.

During the American Revolution, the Ohio Territory was an area of contention for colonists and Native Americans. Some settlers recognized the region as a bastion of opportunity that was theirs for the taking. Many Native Americans felt deceived by the American colonists' breaking of the Proclamation of 1763. Soon the Native Americans became very sympathetic toward the British cause. Many Native Americans saw the vast stretches of land they considered their home and hunting grounds being destroyed by the methods used by the new eastern transplants to establish their homes. These Native Americans witnessed land they had farmed, hunted on, and lived within for centuries, changed forever by the new settlers. Settlers stripped the ground, showing little to no regard for the surrounding environment.

Trees that were hundreds of years old quickly disappeared, and the new settlers replaced them with open fields. By the end of the American Revolution in 1783, Green Township was still an untamed wilderness, but things were about to change. While the founding fathers were meeting back east to create a new American government, a few pioneers were making their way to the Ohio Territory utilizing the Cumberland Gap and the newly organized territory of Kentucky. Word began to trickle back east about the beauty and abundance of the Ohio Country. One of these individuals who heard of the potential for growth and profit was a man named Benjamin Stites. Stites made several trips to the area down the Ohio River and decided to enlist the help of others in his quest to settle and profit from this territory.

John Cleves Symmes was essential to Green Township's history, which was also synonymous with the settlement of Cincinnati. Symmes was a delegate to the Continental Congress and judge from New Jersey in 1788 when he acquired over 311,000 acres from Congress.[2] In November of that year, a contemporary of Symmes that he had convinced to make their way west, named Benjamin Stites brought a small group of settlers down the Ohio River. They made their way down the river on flatboats and settled in what is today the eastern suburb of Cincinnati called Columbia-Tusculum. Stites and his settlers named their settlement Columbia. In December that year, Robert Patterson and Mathias Denman led the second group of settlers down the Ohio River. They landed at what is now the Public Landing area on the riverfront of Cincinnati. They named their tiny settlement Losantiville. Finally, in 1789, Symmes made his way down the river with the third group of settlers and landed west of the Losantiville site. Symmes named his settlement North Bend for the steep northern bend the river takes on its way west to the Mississippi River. [3]

The settlement was slow in the territory known as the Northwest Territory, of which Ohio was part, due in part to the hostile actions taken toward American settlers by the Native Americans in the area. In 1790, due to increasing fears of the

---

[2] Silberstein, Iola, *Cincinnati, Then and Now*, Cincinnati, League of Women Voters, 1982 10.

[3] Silberstein, 9-10

Shawnee, President George Washington directed the United States Army to erect a fort to protect U.S. citizens settling in the area. Settlers built Ft. Washington to hold over 200 troops and serve as a warning to all Native Americans considering attacks. Due to the fort's presence, the settlement remained along the riverfront. Settlers stayed there after a pioneer outpost called Fort Dunlap (in what would later be named Colerain Township) was attacked near the Great Miami River in January 1791. Shawnee forces led by Simon Girty and reportedly Blue Jacket, numbering over 300, surrounded and laid siege to the fort, which federal soldiers and an officer defended from Ft. Washington.[4]

Green Township Established

Before Green Township could support permanent settlers, the Congress of the United States set up rules for governing and dividing what people called public lands. The Land Ordinance of 1785 created the guidelines for the shape and character of Green Township. According to the Land Ordinance, the land was to be divided into six-mile, square townships created by lines running north and south and intersecting at right angles with east/west lines. Townships were to be arranged in north/south rows called ranges. Most townships were subdivided into 36 one-mile square sections. Each range, Township, and section were to be numbered in a

---

[4] Kramb, Edwin A. *Buckeye Battlefields*. Springboro, OH: Valhalla Press, 2006.

regular, consistent sequence. [5] Unlike most of Ohio, the Symmes Purchase was a mixture of townships divided differently.

In 1788 the Symmes purchase was settled by new residents and split into three distinct townships: Columbia, Losantiville, and Miami. These three vast townships encompassed almost all of what is now modern Hamilton County between the Great and Little Miami Rivers. These three areas were formed from the three original settlements of the Symmes Purchase. These three areas were: Columbia, settled by Benjamin Stites in November 1788; Losantiville, settled in late December 1788; and North Bend, established by John Cleves Symmes in 1789. The Green Township we know today had its roots in portions of the original Miami and Losantiville townships. Losantiville became known as Cincinnati Township after the Governor of the Northwest Territory, Arthur St. Claire, visited Losantiville and renamed it Cincinnati. Another reason for St. Claire's visit was the establishment of a county, which they named Hamilton, in honor of the current Treasury Secretary and Revolutionary War hero Alexander Hamilton. In 1795, Timothy Symmes, the only full brother of John Cleves Symmes, established South Bend Township to accommodate South Bend, the brand new settlement close to what is now Anderson Ferry. Because of its central location, John Cleves Symmes touted North Bend as the future home of

---

[5] Knepper, Dr. George, *The Official Ohio Lands Book* , Columbus Ohio, Auditor of the State of Ohio Publication, 2002, 13-16

the metropolis of his purchased lands. This idea was supported by a detachment of 21 federal troops stationed there for a short time before the establishment of Fort Washington. Unfortunately, the area grew undesirable when floodwaters forced the abandonment of the settlement to higher ground. As a result, much of the Symmes Purchase remained loosely organized, massive townships, while most of the attention for settlement was given to Cincinnati after the establishment of Ft. Washington. South Bend Township included all of today's Delhi Township and most of Green Township.

Colerain Township claimed small sections of what ended up being today's northern Green Township. Colerain Township was formed in 1794 by the Court of General Quarter Sessions of Peace. These courts were the judicial system for the Northwest Territories. In 1803, Ohio became the 17th state, changing the civil divisions. This is when sources indicate that Hamilton County began to shrink as many newer counties formed from Hamilton County. These more recent counties included Butler and Warren counties to the north and Clermont County to the east. Hamilton County came very close to the shape it is today. From this point, surveyors began carving up Hamilton County into different townships as outlined in the Land Ordinance of 1785. Green Township, labeled within the Symmes Purchase as Fractional Range 2, Township 2, was the only Township created in the Symmes Purchase totaling 36 square miles. The accepted date of creation for Green Township is 1809.

While no known account exists of the first trustees or their meetings, an early source describes the government structure of the beginning of the townships in Hamilton County. The state law stipulated that once a suitable number of men wanted to establish a government, the County Constable must call a meeting, and he helped choose a presiding officer. He was given orders to arrest anyone who disturbed the meeting. Fifteen male taxpayers had to be present, and they, in turn, elected officials by secret ballot. These officials consisted of three or more trustees, two overseers of the poor, three fence viewers, two appraisers of houses, one lister of property, and many land supervisors. In the early history of Green Township, it was not considered an honor to hold office; pay was low, resources were not readily available, and guidance from state officials was non-existent. Due to these conditions, after being elected to office, anyone refusing was fined $5. By 1831 it was reduced to a fine of $2. After 1850, the office salaries increased to be accepted by those nominated.[6]

Today, the Green Township slate of elected officials consists of three township trustees and a fiscal officer. They all run for office using modern political campaigns, and Township residents vote for candidates are at least 18 years old and registered to vote. The trustees appoint any other positions within the township administration, and many other jobs use civil service examinations to produce the best

---

[6] Scully, Henry, ed, *Remember When…Monfort Heights*, Cincinnati Ohio, Monfort Heights Civic Association, 1977, 19

and brightest candidates for possible approval by the township trustees.[7]

Earliest Firefighting Efforts

Records indicate that early firefighting efforts were complicated in Cincinnati and surrounding areas. The first recorded fire in the Cincinnati area was in 1794. This fire was referred to as a "brush" fire, which destroyed over 100 acres of dry timber on the northern fringes of the settlement that would later be named Cincinnati.[8] The city's first fire laws were passed in 1802 in the newly incorporated Cincinnati, and the first fire equipment was purchased for said town.[9] In 1853, Cincinnati City Council authorized the first professional fire service funded by the city.[10] Cincinnati's Fire Department was the first professional fire protection department in the United States. This became the model for many other large cities to copy. Fire protection was not only a safety issue, but it was an insurance issue as well. Insurance rates were rising, and a fire service that was on call and ready at a moment's notice helped ease the financial burden of fire insurance on city residents in the 1800s.

---

[7] Green Township Webpage, (accessed 4/29/2020) http://www.greentwp.org

[8] Kiefer, Kathleen J., *Flying Sparks & Hooves: Prologue;* Cincinnati Historical Society Bulletin, Volume 28 No 2 Summer 1970, 83

[9] Kiefer, 83

[10] Kiefer, 102

Green Township and its rural way of life in the 1800s did not allow for complete safety services like nearby Cincinnati. Green Township's population from its first census in 1810 to 1920 did not rise above 10,000 citizens.[11] Westwood, the first Green Township community to have a volunteer firefighting group, was incorporated as a village in 1868.[12] Westwood was later annexed into the City of Cincinnati in 1896, bringing numerous city services and ammenities, including fire protection to the citizens of Westwood. The Green Township community of Cheviot did not become a village until 1901. Shortly after, in 1912, Cheviot formed its first volunteer firefighting group they named a "volunteer fire militia." This group had 15 initial members to help fight fires in the village of Cheviot.[13]

The distance from Westwood and Cheviot to northern and western Green Township resulted in delays in fire fighting assistance, leaving residents on their own to deal with the threat of fire. Several fires in Green Township history caused quite a lot of damage before the township had full-time fire protection. In 1892, a fire broke out in the roof of the priest's rectory at St. Aloysius Gonzaga church in Bridgetown. A manuscript by the Schaible family details many of the harrowing details of this significant structure fire, which saw many men from

---

[11] Flickinger, Joe; *A Bicentennial History of Green Township: Uncovering a Jewel in the Crown of the Queen City*, Heritage Books 2011, 57

[12] Clarke, S. J. *"Cincinnati, the Queen City, 1788-1912, Volume 2"*. The S. J. Clarke Publishing Company. 1912, 528

[13] Martin, Rich, Klein, Robert, Michel, Roberta; *We Love Cheviot*; Cheviot Historical Society, 2018, 77-78

the surrounding farms rush to the building to help extinguish the flames. While the building was saved, the loss was around $325- about $9,000 in today's dollars. Fortunately, the church had fire insurance, and their policy covered the loss.[14]

A large fire that caused quite a stir in the rural township was the barn fire on the farm of Nicholas Ruebel in 1902. The entire barn was destroyed, along with sixty tons of hay, harnesses, and numerous plows. Ruebel contacted the Westwood Fire Engine of the Cincinnati Fire Department via telephone. Ruebel, a well-known contractor in Hamilton County, set his losses at around $4-5,000, roughly over $150,000 today. The Cincinnati Enquirer article that covered the fire proclaimed that Ruebel had just canceled one of his insurance policies on his property eight days before.[15]

Another fire heavily damaged the Martin Zimmerman Blacksmith shop before the Cincinnati Fire Department Westwood station was able to respond in 1908. Blacksmith Martin Zimmerman and his helper attempted to put out the fire, which started in the shop's basement on Cleves Pike(today's Bridgetown Road). A bucket brigade was formed from a nearby creek, but the fire quickly spread to the Zimmerman house, located 50 feet away, and another neighboring home. The estimated damage was around $3,000, which would be approximately $80,000 in the 21st Century. In

---

[14] Schaible, Charles; *I Was Interested*; Green Township Historical Association Archive; Autobiography, 1972

[15] *Fire: Destroys a Fine Barn on Contractor Ruebels Farm*; Cincinnati Enquirer, January 22, 1902, 7

addition, several volunteers from the bucket brigade that tried to put out the fire suffered severe burns to their skin.[16]

The risk to residents' lives and property was immense heading into the 1920s. There was a slightly higher population jump in Green Township, attributed to the streetcars extending into Westwood and Cheviot. In addition, small pockets of new housing were being built around the township close to Cheviot and Westwood. Citizens led the charge to try to fill in where the township government could not or would not. The earliest form of fire service in Green Township which directly worked with township government was the formation of the Green Township Fire Protective Association in 1928.[17] This organization did not respond to active fires. Instead, it was established as a way for property owners in the unincorporated sections of Green Township to contract with Cheviot for fire services. The association also began negotiating to extend water mains into the unincorporated areas of its members for fighting fires. Under the contracts with Cheviot, the members had the same rights and privileges for fire protection as if they lived in Cheviot. The fire association was so popular that it negotiated fire protection from Cincinnati for the Covedale residents of the southeast portion of the Township throughout the 1930s. The association met at Focke's Tavern, located next to St Aloysius at the

---

[16] Flames: Threatened Bridgetown. Cincinnati Fire Department Called To the Scene--Two Residences *Cincinnati Enquirer (1872-1922);* Sep 5, 1908;

[17] First Call: Fire Protection by Member of Township Association Made Christmas Day; *Western Hills Press*; December 27th, 1929

intersection of Cleves Pike(Bridgetown Rd) and Church Lane.[18] Later in its existence, the Association would often act as a "salvage corps," offering members an opportunity to have extra help to salvage materials from their property after a fire.

Heading into the 1940s, the population of the unincorporated areas of Green Township experienced small, steady growth. World War II did not hamper efforts at small pockets of housing being built around the township. As WWII drew into 1944, a civil defense group in Green Township met regularly and began to discuss the problems that fires were causing in unincorporated Green Township. That year would see Green Township and these civic-minded men venture into fire protection, which would help protect the township's citizens throughout its post-WWII baby boom years.

---

[18] Annual Meeting of Green Township Fire Protective Association Next Monday; *Western Hills Press*, January 10th, 1930

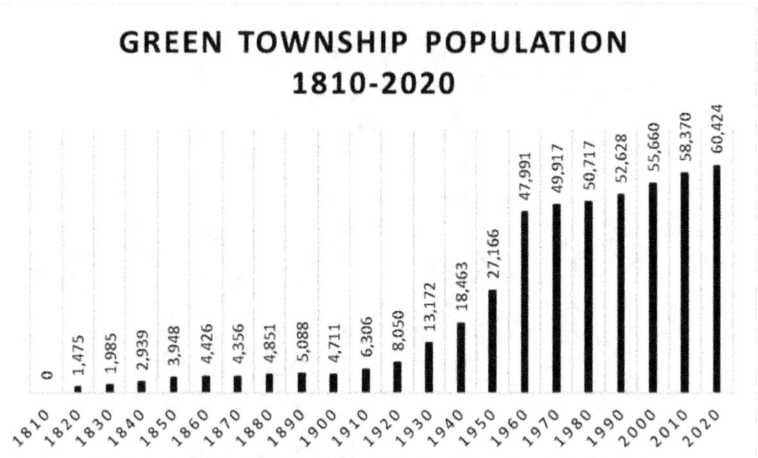

The US Census data shows how small Green Township's population was throughout the 1800s. Supporting a fire department was impossible until the population grew in the 1920s and 1930s. (Courtesy Green Township Historical Association)

The Scheidt house, stood on Ebenezer Road, close to the intersection of Taylor, Bridgetown, and Ebenezer roads. This building would be converted into the Shady Lawn Tavern, which was a key meeting place for the fledgling Mack Volunteer Fire Department. This building was eventually torn down and replaced by a bank. (Courtesy Green Township Historical Association)

This photo shows the Bross Farm, located at what is today the busy intersection of Bridgetown and Ebenezer Roads. This image looks southwest. The house and barn in the picture would have been located right across the street from the original firehouse on Bridgetown Road. The date of this photo is estimated to have been taken in the 1920s. (Courtesy Green Township Historical Association)

The Markland General Store, located at the northeast corner of the intersection of Bridgetown, Taylor, and Ebenezer roads. The small general store in this image, estimated from the 1930s, shows just small the rural area's population was. (Courtesy Green Township Historical Association)

An Honor Roll sign outside the Markland General Store from the mid-1940's. Signs like these were common in rural areas to show off the civic pride of the area's residents who were fighting in World War II. (Courtesy Green Township Historical Association)

Martin Zimmerman's blacksmith shop on Bridgetown Road, suffered an early devastating fire in Green Township history. The original shop burned down in 1908, despite efforts to extinguish the fire, including a "bucket brigade," and firefighters from a neighboring department failed. The structure was rebuilt later that year. (Photo courtesy Green Township Historical Association)

Chapter Two:
Fulfilling a Dire Need in Green Township

At the Beginning of the 1940's, Green Township slowly emerged from the grips of the Great Depression, just as the rest of the Cincinnati area had. Men and women from Green Township participated in the Works Progress Administration, Civilian Conservation Corps, and other New Deal job-creation programs to help drag the country out of the grips of the financial depression experienced by many in the 1930s. Then, on December 7th, 1941, the United States was attacked by the Japanese air and naval forces in Pearl Harbor, Hawaii. The next day, the United States declared war on Japan and their allies, Germany and Italy. The push to mobilize for war inspired many township young men to enlist to serve their country. The citizens of Green Township found many ways to support their fathers, brothers, uncles, and cousins in the European and Pacific theatres. Scrap metal drives, Victory Gardens, tire recycling, and even nylon for parachutes were donated by the people of Green Township for the war efforts. The long brutal war effort saw everyone unite for one cause- victory. When April 1945 saw the surrender of Germany to Allied Forces, hope sprang eternally. When Japanese forces surrendered in September 1945 after two nuclear bombs were dropped on their cities, rebuilding Europe and Japan began in earnest, and converting the U.S. economy to a peacetime economy would start immediately.

When Franklin Roosevelt signed into law the GI Bill in June 1944, the impact on the country after the war was tremendous. The Veterans Administration would carry out the law's main ideas. Those ideas included veteran education or training, loan guarantees for homes, farms, businesses, and unemployment pay. The GI Bill would be one of many reasons for the rise of suburbs in the post-war decades. Farms and farming communities that surrounded significant urban areas would be transformed into areas now known as suburbs. Farmers were more than happy to sell for a high price to developers who turned sometimes struggling farms into sprawling subdivisions, each divided lot containing a house, attached garage, and fenced-in yard. Some houses had two bedrooms. Others had three and four bedrooms. On-street parking was plentiful, and traffic was limited to most residents and visitors. Numerous families moved into these new housing developments, backed by the GI Bill and post-war prosperity. Green Township was one of many rural communities surrounding Cincinnati that experienced tremendous growth post-WWII.

The growth that Green Township experienced did not happen entirely post-WWII. Historical records show that the township still had small pockets of streets that experienced growth during the 1940s. Streets added 10-15 homes, often laid out on small patches of land carved from large farms. In addition, Green Township census data shows a slight jump in population from a little over 15,000 residents in 1930 to close to 20,000 residents in 1940. This jump in population was enough to spur a look at safety services in the township.

In 1942, Green Township Trustees contracted directly with the City of Cheviot for emergency services, including fire protection. They also negotiated contracts with the Delhi Volunteer Department for the extreme southern sections of the township, commonly known as Covedale. The Groesbeck Department also held a contract for the northern areas of Green Township, which included White Oak and Monfort Heights. These early contracts often paid a flat fee per emergency run. Several other departments would also assist in mutual aid situations, including the Westwood station in the Cincinnati Fire Department and the Miamitown Department. However, Green Township would not have its fire department until a group of civic-minded individuals met and began to discuss how to provide the Township with its fire and rescue department.

As WWII raged into 1944, a group of members from the Civil Defense Unit in the Township began discussing how to ensure Green Township had its own fire and rescue service. Losses from recent fires, fear of WWII making its way to American soil, and response times from surrounding community departments were all concerns that spurred the conversations. In June 1944, the Mack Volunteer Fire Department was established to protect the Mack community of Green Township. The first meetings for the fledgling department were held in the meeting room of the Shady Lawn Tavern on Ebenezer Road, which would end up being located about one block north of the first firehouse. The first officers were: William Stroschen Jr., President; Ralph Carle, Vice-President; John Soaper, Secretary; Joe Lingers, Treasurer; Walter Stroschen, Sergeantat-Arms; and William Neiheisel, Sam Zaeske, and Ed Luhrman, as trustees.[19]

According to the Mack Fire Inc archives, the first years of the department's existence was a flurry of activity, including writing by-laws, negotiating for property for a firehouse, and innumerable fundraisers to fund the young fire department. In the first years of the department, numerous raffles and festivals in the summer and turkey shoots and raffles in the fall were held to acquire equipment and property. In early 1945, the Mack Civic Association, an organization that spearheaded community projects, helped present several social functions to benefit the early MVFD. Socials, bake sales, and meetings with the South Avenue School PTA(South Avenue School later merged with Dent School to create the current Springmyer Elementary in the Oak Hills School District), Wilke Community Church, Boy Scouts, and Girls Scouts helped early efforts at raising funds for the Mack department.[20] In May 1945, the MVFD held its first big festival at the Harvest Home Park in Cheviot. The festival, which featured a "pony track," carnival games, dancing, and plate sandwiches, was organized to raise money for a new proposed fire station on Cincinnati-Louisville Pike(today's Bridgetown Rd). This station would have entrances on Cincinnati-Louisville Pike(Bridgetown Rd) and Taylor Roads.[21] These festival proceeds enabled the department to

---

[19] Archives of Mack Fire Inc, November 2020, Organization Meeting Minutes, Formerly Known as Mack Volunteer Fire Department, Mack Fire Headquarters, Cincinnati Ohio

[20] Archives of Mack Fire Inc. Organization Meeting Minutes

[21] Archives of Mack Fire Inc.. Organization Meeting Minutes

construct the new firehouse on a section of the old Bross Farm on Cincinnati-Louisville Pike next to the Steinman Garage in June 1945.[22] Today, a garden is maintained by volunteers on the site of the old Steinman Garage. Mack Fire Inc helped secure funding for this garden. Work continued through the rest of 1945 and throughout 1946 using volunteer labor from the community at the firehouse. The department also accepted monetary donations as well as equipment and other supplies. These donations allowed the department to acquire a new pumper and an emergency car. The Cheviot Civilian Defense Corps also donated a civil defense siren to Mack. This siren sat on top of Cheviot City Hall and would find a new home on the new fire house in Mack.[23] In September 1947, the dedication of the new Mack Firehouse took place with numerous local and county dignitaties attending.[24] Due to the ever-expanding volume of calls to the volunteer department, they expanded their recently completed firehouse in June 1949.[25] This would be the first of many planning meetings, fundraising ventures, and construction and additions to the Mack Department buildings over the next few decades.

Old Association Fades to the Past.

The Green Township Fire Association, which was organized in 1928 as a collaborative effort to negotiate fire service from organized departments in Cheviot and other neighboring communities for the residents of Green Township, made plans to donate

---

[22] Archives of Mack Fire Inc. Organization Meeting Minutes

[23] Ibid

[24] Ibid

[25] Ibid

their remaining money in their treasury since MVFD was now handling many calls in Green Township. The association had not functioned since 1944, when the Green Township trustees started assuming the cost of fires attended to by neighboring departments. The remaining $1,000 was donated to the Mack Department, and the old Fire Association disbanded.[26] In late 1950, the organization's donation to the Mack department to purchase new hoses for their trucks was complete, and the association dissolved at a meeting held at the Mack firehouse.[27]

The Baby Boom Years

Green Township experienced exponential growth during the 1950s. As stated before, farms transformed into housing developments rapidly, increasing calls for service from the volunteer fire department. The Mack department made numerous calls for house fires, grass fires, and runs for traffic accidents. In 1950, a landfill on South Road caught fire, necessitating the Mack firefighters to be called to the scene to help extinguish the flames.[28] This would not be the last time this landfill saw Mack firefighters respond to fires.

The MVFD spent numerous hours training its volunteers on how to use new equipment. As a result of the population growth in the township, the MVFD signed a flat-rate contract with the Green Township Trustees. This new contract granted all township

---

[26] Ibid

[27] Ibid

[28] Ibid

residents protection from the MVFD.[29] The only area not covered by Mack was the Covedale area, where the Delhi Volunteer Fire Department provided service due to their proximity.[30]

The biggest news from this contract was the announcement that Mack would build a second station in Monfort Heights to protect the township's northern residents.[31] During the early 1950s, Monfort Heights saw many new homes constructed, necessitating the new fire station. Add in the offices of Green Townships' Trustees and small administrative staff leasing office space in the new addition built onto the Mack firehouse; space was sorely needed. Green Townships Trustees met at The Wagon Wheel Cafe at the intersection of Bridgetown Road, Race Road, and Glenway Avenue and before that at Fockes Tavern at Church and Bridgetown roads.[32] This would have been standard practice in the area since many of the schools and other public buildings at the time would not have been large enough to hold a crowd, should one gather for a meeting.

The new Monfort Heights station occupied an old roadway maintenance building on North Bend Road just south of West Fork Road. The township provided the equipment bays rent-free, and MVFD provided a pumper and trained volunteers from the community to serve. In 1957, the Green Township Trustees acquired their first administration building on Cheviot Road. The township provided enough

---

[29] Archives of Mack Fire Inc., Reports to Green Township Trustees

[30] Archives of Mack Fire Inc. Organizational Meeting Minutes

[31] Ibid

[32] Ibid

space for the Mack department to have two equipment bays and allowed the fireman to remodel other parts of that building for a meeting room, office, and first aid room. This station would serve the northern sections of the township until 1964, when the present property on West Fork Road was purchased.

The 1960's and More Growth

Green Township experienced sustained growth and change in the 1960s. The prosperity of the 1950s allowed the 1960s to usher in larger subdivisions, more cars, and more people. The roads, which accommodated more animals than people 25 years ago, now welcomed more cars and the traffic delays that came with them. As more people, businesses, and homes came to the area, the number of fundraising activities, training, and emergencies the MVFD participated in also grew.

The Monfort Heights station was finished in October 1966 at the corner of Audro and West Fork. The new station provided four equipment bays for the fire department's efforts to serve and protect northern Green Township's citizens. The opening ceremony brought State Fire Marshal George Schlotterbeck, US Congressman Donald Clancy, Cincinnati Fire Chief Bert Lugannani, Hamilton County Commissioners, the Hamilton County Sheriff, Green Township Trustees, and members of the Mack Civic Association and White Oak Improvement Association.

The MVFD faced one of its most significant emergencies up to that point in its history when the Cheviot Tire Company on Bridgetown Road, close to the intersection with Frondorf Ave, caught fire in September 1962. Shortly after WWII, the business was established as a tire retreading business for the Sentinel-Signal Corporation and the local distributor of Seiberling Tires. The loss of tires alone was estimated at over $12,000 in 1962, roughly $107,000 in the early 21st Century.[33] Overall, the loss of the building, machinery, and other equipment set a total loss at over $225,000, which in the early 21st Century would be worth well over $5.8 million. The MVFD was assisted by Cheviot Fire Department, Delhi Fire Department, and others sending extra firefighters to staff the firehouses that were attending to the fire. In addition, the Cheviot Police Department and Hamilton County Sheriff Deputies assisted by helping control traffic and the large crowd of onlookers to the fire. The blaze took several hours to contain, hampered by falling walls on the west and rear ends of the building. The fire was estimated to have started around 2 pm, with the Mack firefighters staying on-site until well past midnight. The Delhi Volunteer Fire Department sent their bulldozer to help scatter the remaining piles of simmering tires so the firefighters could fully extinguish the flames. The State Fire Marshal attributed the cause of the fire to an electric spark igniting paint fumes.[34]

Auxiliary Groups Help Round out Service

The MVFD had several arms of service that helped round out service and supported emergency

---

[33] Archives of Mack Fire Inc. Reports to Green Township Trustees
[34] Ibid

crews' efforts. In May 1955, the Mack Ladies Auxiliary was formed. The group's purpose was to bring the wives, mothers, and widows of active and honorary members of the department together to act as a fundraising group and support during fire and rescue services by the department. By 1962, the group made its first sizeable donation to the MVFD, over $1,000 for use by the department. By 1969 the group was also raising enough money to purchase uniforms for each member of the MVFD. The group also held cookouts for the members of the MVFD and purchased more equipment such as compressors, masks, several Plectron radios, and more furniture for the new Monfort Heights station.

The group experienced its most significant test on April 3rd, 1974, when a tornado that was part of a massive "super outbreak" of storms hit Mack and Dent. The Ladies Auxiliary set up at the Mack station to provide food, shelter, and console the victims of this destructive weather event. Many days were spent cooking food for the victims and the firefighters during rescue and cleanup efforts.

Several members of the Ladies Auxiliary went on to take Emergency Medical Technician training and joined the MVFD in 1975. The group also provided refreshments at the opening of the Covedale Station in 1977 and raised money for several vehicles for the department in the 1970s. This group served the department well into the 1980s.[35] Through their efforts, the MVFD could grow and be supported by their efforts for the community. This group's valuable service to the

---

[35] Archives of Mack Fire Inc., Organizational Meeting Minutes

department is still recounted by many veteran Mack firefighters today.

"Hello, Mack Fire Department"

In the late 1940s through the early 1980s, when you had an emergency in Green Township, 911 was not the number to call; M01-6761 was the number that would be called for help. The phone would then ring in the private residences of firefighters. The wives of the firefighters who answered were known as telephone operators. Later they would take the title of dispatcher. The women would take the call, write down the information, then call the firefighters' homes to respond to the emergency. The siren on top of the firehouse would also be activated to alert the firefighters. Later, a Plectron radio system was installed, which put a radio in every firemen's house. The operators would be on duty from 6 am until 8 pm when the night volunteer shift came on duty. Two "nightmen" would sleep at the firehouse and take emergency calls at night. Many MVFD members would say that these operators were the unsung heroes of the department. The MVFD operators were disbanded in the early 1980s when the MVFD joined the Hamilton County Dispatch System.[36]

The MVFD showcased its importance through safety and emergency services and civic service. This reputation would only increase as the township population swelled in the 1970s. More demands, more training, and more emergency runs meant

---

[36] Archives of Mack Fire Inc., Organizational Meeting Minutes

changes for the department going through the next few decades of service to the community.

Signs like this one advertised for various civil defense groups during World War II. Many of these groups helped organize scrap drives, "blackout" drills, and air raid drills in homes and schools to practice in case of enemy attack. Members of one of these groups formed MVFD. (Courtesy Green Township Historical Association)

The first firehouse was constructed in 1945 on Bridgetown Road on a small portion of the old Bross Farm. Notice the sign in front states, "Volunteer Help Wanted: Mack O Fire Dept." (Photo courtesy Mack Fire Inc.)

Many of the charter members of the MVFD posing in front of the original firehouse on Bridgetown Road in 1947. (Photo courtesy Mack Fire Inc)

This image from the late 1940s shows the newly constructed MVFD fire house on Bridgetown Road proudly displaying its fire apparatus for the public. (Photo courtesy Mack Fire Inc.)

The first "rolling stock" of the MVFD on display in the late 1940s or early 1950s. (Photo courtesy Mack Fire Inc.)

Men posing for a photograph in 1949 after a training exercise behind the new fire station on Bridgetown Road. Several houses on Taylor Rd are visible behind the men, located behind the firehouse. (Photo courtesy Mack Fire Inc.)

This image shows one of the many fairs and other social events held by the MVFD to raise money for their operations and equipment needs. This photo shows a fair held at the original firehouse in 1949. (Photo courtesy Mack Fire Inc.)

This photo, which dates from the late 1940s, shows a Mack Volunteer posing in one of the rescue vehicles in the early department. (Photo Courtesy Mack Fire Inc)

This image, from 1951, shows the firefighters and the chief modeling their helmets and firefighters' jackets. (Photo courtesy Mack Fire Inc.)

One of many members' meals served in the firehouse in 1953. These gatherings allowed the MVFD members to gather and eat in a social setting. (Photo courtesy Mack Fire Inc.)

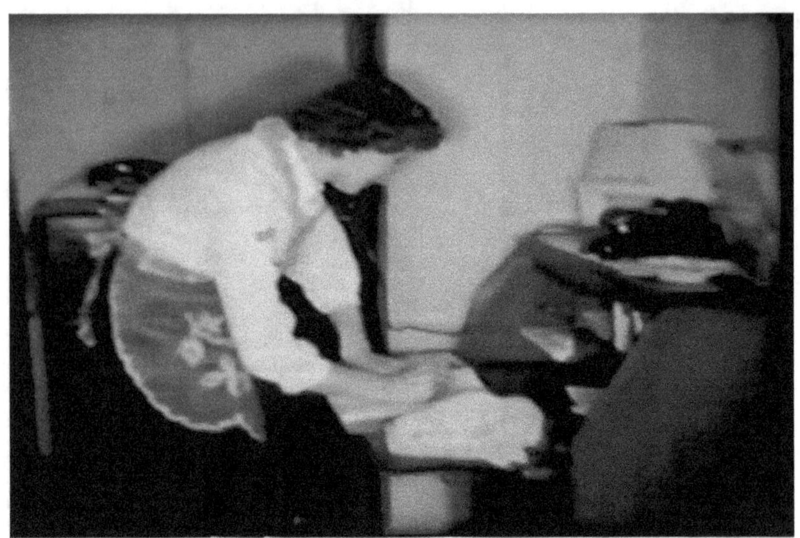

A Mack Dispatcher is writing down essential information from a call to the volunteer department before sounding the siren atop the firehouse on Bridgetown Road. These volunteer dispatchers served the MVFD until the early 1980s, when the department joined Hamilton County's dispatch system. (Photo courtesy Mack Fire Inc.)

The Mack Volunteer Fire Department members posing in 1954 in front of the recently expanded Mack fire station on Bridgetown Road . (Photo courtesy Mack Fire Inc.)

Crowds gathering on Bridgetown Road to watch the MVFD fight the Cheviot Tire fire, which was the most significant emergency the young fire department had to handle up to that point. In the photo's background is the old C & O Train Trestle and Wagon Wheel Cafe. (Photo courtesy Mack Fire Inc.)

This photo shows the Cheviot Tire Company on fire. Cheviot and Delhi's departments assisted the MVFD due to the blaze's size. Unfortunately, the building was a total loss. (Photo courtesy Mack Fire Inc.)

This photo shows the bulldozer brought over to the Cheviot Tire blaze by the Delhi Fire Department. The bulldozer helped spread around the rubble from the building so the MVFD could target hotspots with water from their hoses. (Photo courtesy Mack Fire Inc.)

This image shows the original Monfort Heights Station in 1954, shortly after it opened on North Bend Rd in an old Township Road Maintenance building. This would serve the department until 1957 when the second Monfort Heights Station opened in the new Green Township Administration complex on Cheviot Rd 1957. (Photo courtesy Mack Fire Inc.)

This photo shows the Monfort Heights Station with their vehicles after it was relocated from North Bend Rd to behind the new township administration building on Cheviot Rd in 1957. (Photo courtesy Doug Witsken)

This areal image shows John Foster Dulles Elementary School in the Oak Hills District with smoke billowing from inside the building. A small fire broke out in a storage closet on Friday evening, May 9th, 1969. Thanks to the quick work of the MVFD, the fire was extinguished with minor damage to the building, and the students missed no school. (Photo courtesy Mack Fire Inc.)

Onlookers view the wreckage of a small plane that crashed on Taylor Road near the intersection with Powner Road on September 27, 1961. A small single-engine airplane with two passengers crash-landed in the small creek following Taylor Road. MVFD responded to the crash, further testing the volunteer's skills in search and recovery efforts. Skills like these would become standard for the men and women of the department to practice and be ready to use. (Photo courtesy Mack Fire Inc.)

Chapter Three:
A Stellar Reputation

As the post-war boom of the 1950s and 1960s sustained itself into the 1970s, the MVFD continued to meet the needs of the growing community of Green Township. The township continued to grow by massive numbers, according to census figures. Green Township reached over 40,000 residents in the 1960s. Newer streets and housing helped push these numbers closer to 50,000 into the 1970s. As a result, places where the public gathered, were bursting at the seams. The Oak Hills Local School District, formed in 1956 by the consolidation of the Bridgetown, Green Township (Springmyer School), and Delhi elementary school districts, would construct new elementary school buildings and add on to Oak Hills High School multiple times through these decades. These buildings would quickly be filled with the continuing influx of new residents. In addition, unique infrastructure needs were beginning to be addressed, such as widening roads, installing sewers, and improving traffic flow with modern traffic signals were only several of the many changes made to this rapidly growing community. The MVFD shone like a beacon of safety to the community's residents through all the hustle and bustle of a rapidly evolving area. The MVFD's numerous calls and emergency runs gave them a stellar reputation for its firefighting, rescue abilities, and professionalism.

Cadets Program for the Future

Members of the MVFD were becoming acutely aware of the need for more recruits to keep their shifts fully staffed. So, in 1967, Chief Don

Schlensker oversaw the creation of a cadet program for the department. The purpose was to create interest in young people in the township between the ages of 16 and 17 to become part of the fire service. The department appointed Captain Bob Weitzel as the instructor for the program, which, when completed, allowed these young men and women the opportunity to join the Mack Department at the age of 18. The first four recruits of the program were Ray Gemmell Jr., Gary Juengling, Hal Welge, and Ed Wortman. All four of the original recruits went on to work in the fire department.

The training for the cadets was held once a month for two hours. The training consisted of knowing where the various pieces of equipment were located on both pumpers and rescue trucks. The instruction included how to tie knots and adequately use the fire equipment. Each member was given a hand-me-down rubber raincoat, old boots, and a hard hat. The cadets were required to wear this equipment anytime they were training at the firehouse. In addition, the cadets were tested on items such as properly loading hoses, rolling hoses, and running various equipment. The cadets would be required to show their school report cards to the chief, and if they did not maintain passing grades, they were suspended from the program until they could reach passing.

The cadets were not allowed to fight any actual fires but were allowed in the firehouse if the siren sounded to assist with cleaning and storing equipment when the fireman arrived back at the station. As a result, several cadets have gone on to high positions in the department, including Hal

Welge, the last chief of the MVFD, and Scott Souders, the third full-time chief of the Green Township Fire and Emergency Medical Service.[37]

Another First-Paramedic Service

The MVFD was adding more services and options for the residents of Green Township throughout the population boom years that were the 1970s. One of the most extensive additions to the department came in March 1976 with the addition of an all-volunteer paramedic unit. Fifteen volunteers took the near-300 hours of training after their day jobs and did their clinical training on weekends. The cost for the training and equipment came from the passage of a township fire tax levy several years before. As a result, MVFD became the first volunteer fire department in Hamilton County to offer paramedic service. Hamilton County Communications and Mack dispatchers knew the paramedic unit as "Medic 1".[38] Including a paramedic service allowed the MVFD to stand as an example to other fire departments for providing extensive life-saving crews to an increasingly growing population. In addition, increasing numbers of residents meant more emergency runs and increasingly more complex medical conditions for the men and women of the MVFD to work to save. As a result, the MVFD earned its reputation as one of the best around, that residents could count on when the time came for emergency care.

---

[37] Archives of Mack Fire Inc., Organizational Meeting Minutes
[38] Ibid

Disaster Strikes

April 3, 1974, would go down in history as one of the worst natural disasters in Green Township's modern recorded history. The events of that day not only changed many of the safety procedures that fire and rescue personnel used but also changed the systems that the National Weather Service employed to provide early warning to the residents of neighborhoods and cities around the United States.

The weather system that damaged Green Township and surrounding communities, including Sayler Park and Xenia, Ohio, was dubbed the "1974 Super Outbreak" by the National Weather Service.[39] This weather system wreaked havoc across 13 states and saw 148 tornadoes, 335 deaths, and more than 6,000 injuries. The Xenia tornado hit several neighborhoods in that community around 4 pm. It rated an F-5 on the Fujita Scale, a measurement used to measure the size and damage potential of a tornado by the National Weather Service. Around 5:30 pm, an F-5 tornado, the highest rating on the Fujita Scale, originated in Rising Sun, Indiana. The tornado then passed through Kentucky and crossed the Ohio River to severely damage Sayler Park

---

[39] US Department of Commerce, NOAA. n.d. "The Super Outbreak of April 3-4, 1974." www.weather.gov. https://www.weather.gov/iln/19740403.

before entering southern Green Township.[40] Once in Green Township, the tornado followed a path very close to South, Bridgetown, and Ebenezer roads. In a meeting with federal, state, and local elected officials several days later at the Mack fire house on Bridgetown Road, then-chief Robert Weitzel relayed the path of damage the tornado took. The meeting identified the following streets that reported significant damage: South Road, Kildare Drive, Menz Lane, Our Lady of Visitation, Bridgetown Road between Westport and Powner Roads, and many homes in those areas seeing lots of damage. Homes on Taylor Road, Starvue, Springoak, Berauer, Springmyer Drive, Ebenezer, and Hayes Road all saw the damage, as well as Wessleman and Harrison Avenue. Johnson Road also saw damage to its intersection with Reemelin and Haft Roads. Our Lady of Visitation and many homes were damaged, yet it was noted that John Foster Dulles and Springmyer elementary school buildings were miraculously spared.[41] The MVFD worked around the clock to ensure that the township's residents were all accounted for and began search efforts for those who were not. The Red Cross and the Ladies Auxiliary ran comfort stations at the Bridgetown Road firehouse for several days for both firefighters and residents. Many Mack volunteer firefighters worked 24-36 hours, ensuring that people and property were kept safe in the storm's aftermath. Numerous veteran firefighters remarked how much

---

[40] Ibid

[41] Archives of Mack Fire inc., Organizational Meeting Minutes

damage they saw and how many houses looked like they had been blown away so easily.

The aftermath of this natural disaster taught many lessons learned by government agencies on how to respond to such catastrophic events. Improvements in communications, warning systems, emergency preparedness, and weather forecasting techniques and equipment have led to increased warning times for emergency personnel, greater public awareness, and more reliable communications to prepare and react to such catastrophic events.[42] The MVFD went above and beyond its motto of "we serve to save." Many Green Township residents still have lasting memories of the heroic actions of the Mack department, their dispatchers, and their Ladies Auxiliary, as well as their cadets who helped wherever they could.

"He was a hell of a man."

The MVFD had built a stellar reputation as one of the best-trained and most dedicated departments in Hamilton County as the 1970s rolled on through the township population boom. Injuries to firefighters were common, and these injuries were tended to, and the firefighters moved on stoic, back to their families and day jobs. However, tragedies

---

[42]US Department of Commerce, NOAA. n.d. "The Super Outbreak of April 3-4, 1974." Www.weather.gov. https://www.weather.gov/iln/19740403.

involving one of their own were an occurrence that was not common to the Mack firefighters. The only on-duty death was of Paul Engelhart in September 1963. Firefighter Englehart died while fighting a grass fire on West Fork Road. He collapsed at the site of the fire, apparently from the dense smoke and heat. A veteran of World War II, and an electrician, Firefighter Englehart left behind a wife and two children.[43] All the members of the Mack firehouses in Bridgetown and Monfort Heights mourned his death. His funeral filled St. Ignatius Church to capacity, with members of the MVFD acting as an honor guard. The procession from the church to St. Joseph Cemetery was accompanied by the Mack Volunteer Fire Department, Hamilton County Sheriff's Deputies, and Green Township Constables. Mr. Englehart had been a member of the department since 1954.

The Beverly Hills Supper Club was the place to see and to be seen in Cincinnati during the 1960s and 70s. Major performers from across the country would make the Southgate, Kentucky supper club a stop on their national tours. On Memorial Day weekend in May 1977, George Zorick, his wife, and several family members, including his father and aunt, attended the club to see singer John Davidson. When a fire broke out and evacuation efforts began, George and his wife made it out of the building. But George, believing his father, aunt, and other patrons were trapped inside, went back into the club to help them escape the growing smoke and flames.

---

[43] Archives of Mack Fire Inc., Organizational Meeting Minutes

Unfortunately, Zorick, his father, his aunt, and over 165 people perished in the fire. In 1976, Zorick had recently been promoted to Captain in the MVFD. He was a truck driver for the Kroger Company and left behind a wife and three young children. Captain Zorick died a hero at the club, using his fire training to help others trapped inside escape. On its way to burial in Vine Street Cemetery, Captain Zorick's flag-draped casket was carried in the hose bed of a Mack fire pumper escorted by Mack firefighters and equipment past the main firehouse on Bridgetown Road. The procession was saluted by the Mack members operating the station. Mack fireman saluted the procession as it passed the station. The Covedale station is dedicated to the memory of Captain Zorick, who was described by an unnamed firefighter to a Western Hills Press reporter in 1977 as "a hell of a man."[44]

Protecting Southern Green Township

Southern portions of Green Township share a border with the City of Cincinnati and Delhi Township. Delhi Township, established in 1816, was once a part of a larger township that, along with Green Township, was named South Bend Township. By the 1920s, the population had risen to the point that the Green Township Fire Association had negotiated rates for emergency runs with Cheviot for Bridgetown. Mack residents negotiated with the Cheviot Fire Department and Cincinnati Fire

---

[44] "Mack Fire Department Escorts Fellow Firefighter George Zorick III," *Western Hills Press*, June 8, 1977.

Department for emergency protection in the southern end of Green Township for a neighborhood that was, by the 1930s, called "Covedale."[45] This arrangement lasted until 1942 when Green Township trustees subcontracted with Delhi Townships Volunteer Fire Department for fire protection in the southern end of Green Township. Like many other agreements with surrounding fire departments, this contract paid on a per "call answered." Therefore, Delhi's Department received a flat rate per call they answered in Green Township. The arrangement lasted until January 1st, 1976, when the MVFD and Green Township trustees declined to renew the contract with Delhi. As a result, Mack provided all fire and emergency services to the entire township for the first time in the department's history.[46]

In 1975, a fire levy was passed by the residents of Green Township. The MVFD also implemented a paramedic unit, requiring more equipment, training, and supplies. These additional items necessitated the fire levy. The levy's passage meant more resources to draw from for equipment purchases and for the potential building of a third fire station in Covedale. The land was purchased on Sylved Road, with several delays pushing the station's construction back to 1977. Finally, the Covedale station was dedicated in October 1977. The Bridgetown Civic Club donated a plaque dedicated to

---

[45] *Western Hills Press*. 1929. *First Call for Fire Protection*, December 29, 1929.

[46] Archives of Mack Fire Inc., Organizational Meeting Minutes

the memory of George Zorick. The station was built to house a pumper and an ambulance.[47]

As the 1970s drew to a close, the MVFD experienced the most significant growth in its history. Significant investments of time, money and resources made the organization the envy of other volunteer departments. The men and women who staffed the department took considerable pride in their service to Green Township's residents. As the 1980s began, a move by the township would change the volunteer fire department in Green Township into the foreseeable future. Green Township government assumed control of fire and rescue operations in 1983. A significant period of township civic history was closing, but a new group emerged from the volunteer department to support the new township department and its operations.

A new name: Mack Fire Inc.

As Green Township began negotiating with MVFD to take over fire and rescue services, Mack's membership knew they wanted to help support the new department as much as possible. Many of the active firefighters and paramedics were set to make the switch to the new township department. A decision was made to transform the volunteer fire

[47] *Cincinnati Enquirer*. 1977. *Mack Firemen to Honor Buddy*, October 1, 1977.

and rescue organization into a fundraising and fraternal organization known a Mack Fire Inc.

As it has been known since 1983, Mack Fire Inc has operated as a not-for-profit fraternal organization made up of predominantly retired Mack volunteer firefighters and their families. Mack Fire runs a fundraising raffle where the proceeds of this event go to purchase equipment and training for the Green Township Fire & EMS that are not usually covered by the department's budget. Since 1983, Mack Fire Inc and its fundraising endeavors have purchased over $400,000 in equipment for the Green Township Fire & EMS department. In addition, they also have several meeting halls in the basement of the original firehouse on Bridgetown Rd, open to all members to use. Membership in Mack Fire Inc is available to all former MVFD members and the successor Green Township Fire & EMS. Social activities at the meeting hall include projects and activities related to fundraising for the Green Township Fire & EMS, organizational meetings, member dinners, and weekly card games such as Euchre.[48]

The fundraising activities that Mack Fire Inc employs include a township-wide raffle. Raffle tickets are sent to every resident of Green Township, who can participate by sending their money and tickets back to Mack Fire. Numerous winners of various prizes are announced every year. This raffle is the primary fundraiser of the year for Mack Fire Inc. Several ongoing items that Mack Fire Inc pays for are smoke detectors and batteries for township

---

[48] Archives of Mack Fire Inc., Organizational Meeting Minutes

residents who are found not to have operating units in their homes. Mack Fire also pays for current Green Township Fire & EMS members to provide CPR training classes on their off-duty days to Green Township residents free of charge. In addition, Mack Fire also pays for training current Green Township Department members to attend out-of-state training for the Fire Honor Guard. This includes their uniforms, props, and all training.[49] These items are provided for with the Mack Fire Inc raffle proceeds.

Mack Fire equipment purchases include thermal imaging equipment to aid firefighters in seeing hotspots in walls and other parts of buildings while fighting a fire. Mountain bikes, EMS supplies for the bikes, and bike uniforms for the current fire and EMS department members were also purchased over the years. This allows greater mobility during festivals and other significant events where trucks and ambulances cannot get in quickly due to crowds. In addition, Mack Fire recently purchased a John Deere Gator utility vehicle and EMS supplies for this vehicle for use by Green Township Fire & EMS at festivals, large gatherings, and other emergencies, off-road instances where emergency crews could not easily access an incident through Fire Trucks or Ambulances.

In addition, a door opening simulator for training purposes, as well as communications equipment, have been purchased by Mack Fire Inc for Green Township Fire & EMS. Because of the fundraising efforts of Mack Fire Inc, this equipment has been acquired quicker so that the department's

---

[49] Archives of Mack Fire Inc., Organizational Meeting Minutes

budgeting process can focus on other items, further saving taxpayers money. Additional items purchased through the years include special gurneys for ambulances, automatic defibrillators, LED lights for trucks, "jaws of life" equipment, pumps to help with flooded basements, ice rescue suits, pulse oximeters, as well as disaster management supplies.[50]

MVFD, and its successor Mack Fire Inc, have been pillars in the community. The people of the township knew that they were safer with MVFD watching over them from 1944 to 1983. From 1983 to today, township residents know that Mack Fire Inc has been supplementing tax funding to support the fire and paramedic services.

---

[50] Archives of Mack Fire Inc., Organizational Meeting Minutes

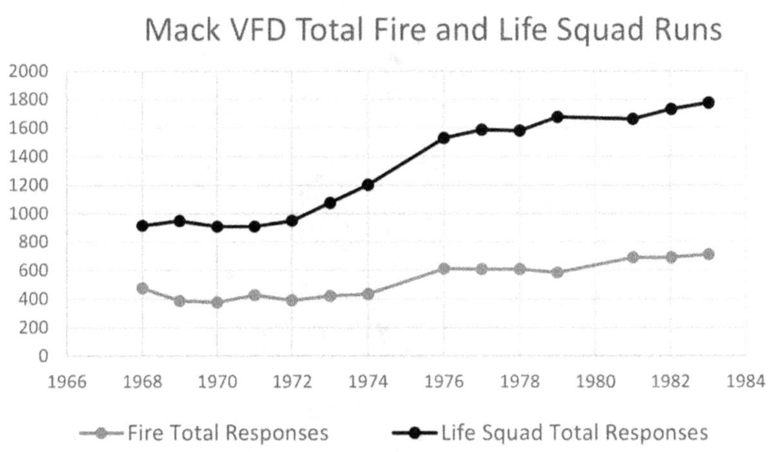

Annual reports of MVFD to the Green Township Trustees from 1968 to 1983 track the calls and runs for the fire squad and EMT's. Records before 1968 could not be found. (Mack Fire Archives)

MVFD firefighter Paul Englehart is the first Mack and Green Township firefighter who died in the line of duty. Englehart, a WWII veteran, and Electrician, died in 1963 while fighting a brush fire. (Photo courtesy Green Township Fire & EMS)

Captain George Zorick of the MVFD. He died while trying to save fellow customers in the Beverly Hills Supper Club fire in Northern Kentucky in May 1977. His service was formally recognized as a line of duty death. (Photo courtesy Green Township Fire & EMS)

Many of the original "Medic 1" members, as the volunteer paramedics of the first paramedic service within Green Township, were known. The Mack Volunteer Fire Department organized and offered paramedic service in 1976. (Photo courtesy Mack Fire Inc.)

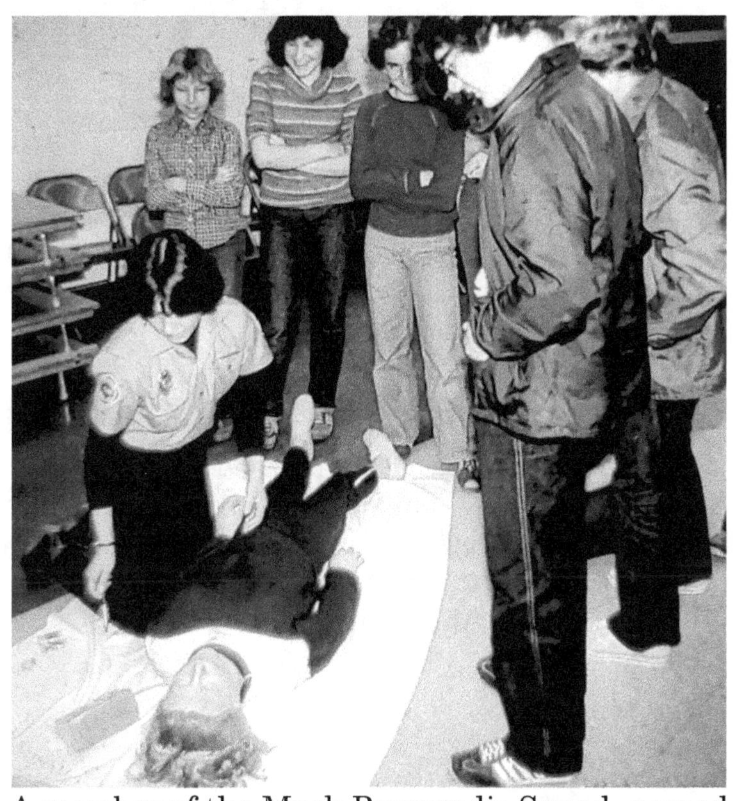

A member of the Mack Paramedic Squad, named "Medic 1," demonstrated first aid techniques to a community group. This demonstration and training would set a standard for the current Green Township Fire & EMS department to meet yearly with its community outreach efforts. (Photo courtesy Don and Arlene Zang)

The April 1974 tornado crossed South and Bridgetown roads. This tornado is considered the biggest natural disaster to hit Green Township in the latter half of the 20th century. (Photo courtesy Mack Fire Inc.)

At 5:46 pm, the Tornado that hit Green Township in April 1974 crossed Bridgetown Road. This image shows the view of the Tornado from the front of the MVFD firehouse on Bridgetown Road. (Photo courtesy Gary Theurer)

The April 1974 tornado after it crossed over Bridgetown Road and Taylor Road and onto Ebenezer Road. This tornado was a part of the "super outbreak" of storms that spawned many strong tornados from Kentucky to Xenia, Ohio. (Photo courtesy Mack Fire Inc.)

Mack Fire Inc. President Ed Wortman presents a check to Green Township Fire & EMS Chief Scott Souders from one of the fundraising endeavors the organization completed to help purchase equipment for the department. (Photo courtesy Mack Fire Inc.)

Members of Mack Fire Inc. pose in front of the original firehouse on Bridgetown Road in 2018. (Photo courtesy Mack Fire Inc.)

Chapter Four: Township Civil Service

As the 1970s drew to a close, the Green Township that many of the original members of the MVFD had known was quickly disappearing. The population continued to grow due to even more subdivisions built throughout Green Township, exceeding 50,000 residents, according to the U.S. Census in 1980.[51] The Oak Hills and Northwest school districts were seeing enormous classes graduate from their school districts due to this influx of population to the area. As a result, roads, sewers, and other public utilities became enormous priorities for Green Township. In 1973, Green Township trustees created a police district and expanded the reach of their small force of constables to that of a full-time police department. The 1975 fire levy passed by the township residents resulted in better equipment and training for the Mack department. Up to this point, volunteers' lights and sirens on their cars were paid for out of their pockets. This levy provided a small stipend for this expense as well. The levy also allowed the Mack department to hire full-time, paid firefighters to serve alongside the volunteers. On January 1, 1980, Bob Weitzel began as the first full-time fire chief. On July 7th, 1980, seven full-time firefighters began with shifts from 7 am to 5 pm. Volunteers still handled all of the open positions and shifts in the department at that time. The first full-time hires for the department were: Jack Bohning, Tom Dietz, Tom Elsbernd, Tom Kotte, Frank Sutton, Ed Thomas, Mark Wagner, and Bob Weitzel as chief.

---

[51] Flickinger, 57

The 1980s continued to bring many changes to the township landscape. For example, the iconic C & O Railroad trestle located at the intersection of Bridgetown, Race, and Glenway avenues was taken down after the C & O Railroad discontinued its freight line through the township. In addition, numerous intersections needed to be widened and reconfigured for more traffic. But the MVFD experienced the most change to its direction and operation in 1983.

"Everyone Felt Mack had to be Preserved."

With the passage of the first fire levy, Green Township officials began to seek more input into allocating the taxpayer's money. For example, in the 1983 rate negotiations with MVFD, the Mack committee did not want full-time firefighters on the township's payroll. But the way the taxes were collected meant that Green Township had to pay the MVFD out of its general fund. While this method was standard practice in the past, changes in accounting rules meant that only township employees could be paid from the township's general fund. So, as a result, Green Township proposed taking over the fire department operation.[52]

Many of the newer members of the MVFD did not want the enormous responsibility of financial management and bookkeeping involved with running the fire department.[53] Mack firefighters could also be held liable if negligence were alleged in the line of duty. Under the auspices of the township

---

[52] Archives of Mack Fire Inc., Organizational Meeting Minutes
[53] Ibid

government, limited immunity could be achieved.[54] While it made sense on paper for the township to take over operations of the fire and emergency services, the sensitivity of making the MVFD a part of the township government was not lost on anyone. The MVFD, by the 1980s, was known as one of the best volunteer departments in the State of Ohio, which served as a model to other departments as to how operations should be done. The strong sense of independent pride and tradition of the MVFD was honored by negotiating to have Mack Fire Inc retain ownership of the two original firehouses on Bridgetown Road and Audro Drive and lease them back to the township for $1 a year. This made sense since the MVFD raised the money and built these two buildings themselves. Those buildings are essential to the members as places to gather and socialize. The Covedale Station, built with fire tax funds, would be owned by the township, as would all other equipment and engines purchased after the passage of the tax levy. Everything purchased before the tax levy would be donated to the township by Mack Fire Inc. It was also decided to name the new department the Green Township-Mack Fire Department [55] On August 23, 1983, many members of the MVFD were sworn in as members of the new Green Township-Mack Fire Department at a Green Township Trustees meeting. Many other members of the Mack Department would be sworn in over the next month who could not attend the township trustee's meeting.

---

[54] Archives of Mack Fire Inc., Organizational Meeting Minutes
[55] Ibid

On April 1st, 1985, the township fire department's volunteer membership ended. At that time, the existing 60-70 volunteers were offered the option to continue working as part-time paid employees of Green Township or resign from their position. Most volunteers chose to stay and were put on a 12-hour shift, which consisted of a day or night shift from 6 to 6 every five days. The full-time firefighters also had their schedules converted from Monday-Friday to 24 hours on, 48 hours off rotation. With this change in scheduling, the department could staff all of their stations 24 hours a day, seven days a week, for all 365 days of the calendar year. Over time, as current part-timers left, new part-time employees without affiliation with Mack Volunteer Fire Department were hired. As of January 2022, the department still maintains four employees who proudly served in the Mack Volunteer Fire Department.

Continued Growth and Change

The momentum that the switchover from a private fire company to an arm of the township form of government continued throughout the rest of the 1980s. After the passage of another fire levy in 1984, the Green Township-Mack Fire Department continued to hire part-time firefighters who worked 12-hour shifts. This was in addition to hiring full-time firefighters and paramedics who worked 24-hour shifts.[56] In addition, the Green Township-Mack Fire Department continued the MVFD tradition of outreach into the community by raising money for a

---

[56] Flickinger, 81

fire simulator for use by local students. The trailer that the house was mounted on would simulate conditions for fire and allow the firefighters to teach the students what they needed to do in case of an emergency in realistic situations.[57] This was in addition to the continued tradition of visits to schools in the township, which MVFD also started.

In 1997, Green Township-Mack Fire Department expanded its officer ranks by promoting three full-time lieutenants. Before this expansion, the chief, assistant chief, and three captains were the only full-time officers. All other fire officers (District Chiefs, Captains, and Lieutenants) were part-time employees who evolved out of their volunteer rank status. Eventually, the department promoted 12 people to full-time lieutenant status, one per station per shift.

The 1990s brought a flurry of activity in response to a population that was continuing to grow and a department that experienced ever-increasing calls for service. In 1991, a recruiting class of over 20 civilians helped increase staffing needs for the next decade. Green Township would also begin adding green striping to the traditionally white fire vehicles that dated back to the MVFD days. This allowed the township department to forge its unique identity while still honoring its past link to the MVFD.

---

[57] Houston, Lynda. 1989. *Green Township Puts Students on Hot Seat. Cincinnati Enquirer*, December 5, 1989.

In 1992, Green Township purchased the old Bob Pulte Oldsmobile car dealership building on Harrison Avenue, located next to the old Dent Drive-In movie theatre complex. The township renovated the old dealership into a sprawling administrative complex for township offices, maintenance garages, police headquarters, and a fourth fire station to ease the burden on the Mack and Monfort Heights stations for the increasing number of calls and runs into the Dent and Taylor Creek areas of the township. In 1993, the fourth fire station was opened, with the headquarters for the fire department also relocated there. This allowed the administrative staff and executive officers to be in the same building as the township staff. That year, the township also purchased the first fully enclosed cab fire truck. Before this new fire engine, all fire trucks had an open cab for the back seat where the firefighters would sit. The new location, equipment, and vehicles helped considerably reduce response times in the Dent-Taylor Creek areas of Green Township.

Green Township-Mack Fire Department established its own Fire Explorers Post in 1993. This group saw many youths from the township join to learn the basics of fire protection and EMS services directly from practicing professionals. This program produced dozens of future department firefighters and paramedics in the township department throughout the 1990s.

The township department further expanded its services when in 1994, the department acquired its first arson dog, Sammy, managed by fire investigator Steve Claytor. When Sammy retired, a second dog named Maverick was brought into the department in 2001. After Maverick came Rudy, who retired in 2020. The program was discontinued after Rudy retired. Funds raised by Mack Fire Inc aided the training and support of the three dogs.

As the 20th century came to a close, the new department was tested, just like the predecessor MVFD was, with a large, significant fire that several businesses would be affected, and like the Cheviot Tire fire from the 1960s, would involve help from many surrounding departments. In 1997, unemployment dipped below 5% for the first time since March 1973, and computers and the internet began to change how everything from businesses to education operated. In Green Township, growth was very apparent along the former path of the C & O Railroad that cut through Green Township. Many businesses with less than ten employees found space to establish themselves and provide services to Green Township's growing population. Mar-Fab Lumber was one of the few businesses around when the railroad tracks were actively used. Established in 1945 as the Marketing and Fabrication Company, the firm specialized in lumber and wood-based products. Wednesday, July 16, 1997, was a day that residents in Green Township remembered because of a significant fire that could have caused more damage if not for the quick action of Green Township's Fire & EMS department. At 1:41 pm., Green Township Fire & EMS crews were dispatched to the businesses on Glenway Avenue for an active fire. The presence of chemicals such as linseed oil, furniture finishers, paint thinners, and other flammable liquids made fighting the fire difficult on top of the searing low 90s July heat. One firefighter was treated for heat exhaustion, and Metro buses were dispatched for the firefighters to cool off in the air-conditioned vehicles. Fire departments from neighboring Cheviot, Delhi and Colerain departments assisted Green Township. The fire, which was thought to be caused by an electrical issue, caused over $2 million worth of damage. Mar-Fab Lumber, an adjoining upholstery company, and a plumbing supply company all sustained damage in the fire. A nearby limousine company was spared after the owner moved their vehicles away from the fire. [58] While the Mar-Fab building was a total loss, the businesses were able to rebound quickly and continue their activities in the following days, thanks in large part to the quick action of the Green Township Fire and EMS Department.[59]

The 2000s brought continued activity and changes to the Township department. A new fire house on Bridgetown Road was constructed at a cost of $1.4 million. This station replaced the original Mack firehouse located at the Five Way intersection of Bridgetown Road, Taylor Road, and Ebenezer Road. The Covedale Station was also rebuilt in 2001 at the cost of $850,000.[60] In 2004, the Green Township Fire Department moved into its brand new Monfort Heights Fire Station on Audro Drive. This new firehouse was built for $1.5 million when it

---

[58] Hoffman, Steve. 1997. *Burned out Firms Rebuilding. Cincinnati Enquirer*, August 12, 1997.

[59] Hopkins, John. 1997. *Blaze guts 3 west-side businesses.* Cincinnati Enquirer, July 17th, 1997.

[60] Forgrave, Reid. 2003. *Township anticipates needs.* Cincinnati Enquirer, November 6, 2003.

was opened.[61] This allows the fire department to operate out of state-of-the-art buildings and accommodate training, living quarters, and exercise areas for the men and women of the department.

The end of the 2000s brought a continued vision of hope and optimism. The department officially changed its name to the Green Township Fire & EMS department in 2005. This name change was brought about by the fact that the makeup of calls and runs that the department was making quickly changed in a burgeoning township. According to the fire department statistics, 78% of emergency calls were now for EMS runs. This trend continued into the 2010s and early 2020s.

---

[61] Flickinger, 82

The 1983 Green Township Trustees meeting, where the township officially established the Green Township-Mack Fire Department. (Photo courtesy Doug Witsken)

In 1994, Green Township-Mack Fire Department acquired Sammy, its first arson investigator dog, who worked with Fire investigator Steve Claytor. Sammy worked for the department from 1994 to 2001. Sammy passed in 2006. (Photo courtesy Green Township Fire & EMS)

Maverick was the second canine investigator acquired by Green Township Fire & EMS. Maverick served from 2001 to 2008. (Photo courtesy Green Township Fire & EMS)

Rudy, pictured here with fire investigator Steve Claytor, served the people of Green Township from 2008 to his retirement in 2020. (Photo Courtesy Green Township Fire & EMS)

Inside of station #54 on Bridgetown Road at Eyrich where the "Mack Station" sign was installed from the original firehouse at the old five-way intersection of Bridgetown, Ebenezer, and Taylor roads. (Photo courtesy Green Township Fire & EMS)

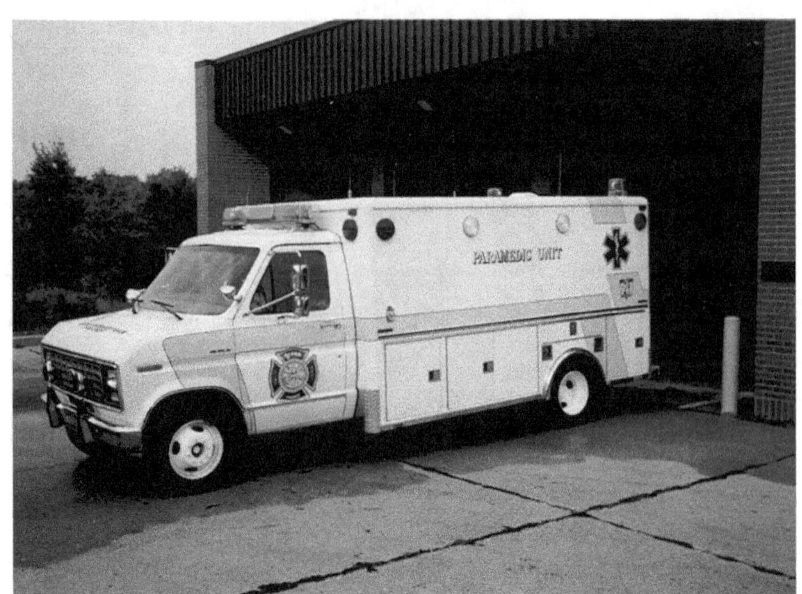

An ambulance in the driveway of the Covedale Station. This vehicle has a Green Township-Mack symbol on the door. This photo was taken sometime in the late 1980s or early 1990s. (Photo courtesy Doug Witsken)

Chapter Five:
Green Township Fire & EMS in the 21st Century

Green Township Fire & EMS continue to serve the township with pride into the 21st century. While fighting fires is still a big part of the training of the men and women employed in the division, one aspect that has grown has been the number of emergency runs in the 21st century. This is indicative of a changing population that requires more varying and complex needs. In 2005, the department's name was changed to reflect one of the many changes to emergency care in Green Township. As a result, the name was changed to the Green Township Fire and EMS. This name change is meant to reflect the changes to the department's calls for service. While fire response calls have continued going up, calls for emergency services requiring EMS personnel have far outpaced fire calls. This trend has continued into the 2020s.

Green Township Fire & EMS has had three full-time paid chiefs since 1980. Bob Weitzel was the first full-time chief from 1980 to 2005. Doug Witsken was the second full-time chief from 2005 until 2017 and the first chief that evolved from working 24-hour shifts. Scott Souders was the third and, as of 2022, current chief. Chief Souders is the first chief to work up through all ranks, from firefighter, Lieutenant, Captain/District Chief, Assistant Chief, and Chief.

The current Green Township Fire & EMS operates four stations. Station 107 is the site of the Covedale Station on Sylved Road, near Muddy Creek. This station works with one pumper, one ambulance, and three people 24 hours a day. Station 54, located on Bridgetown Road next to Eyrich, operates with one pumper, one ambulance, and one

Gator, along with five people at the station 24 hours a day. Station 53 is located on Harrison Ave in the township administration complex. This station houses one ambulance, one pumper(a reserve), one 78 foot ladder truck, one shift commander vehicle, and one reserve ambulance. Six people work at this station 24 hours a day, and the department administration staff are headquartered in this station. The final station is Station 55, Monfort Heights, on Audro Drive. This station houses one pumper and one ambulance and is staffed by five people 24 hours a day. This station also houses a fire investigation unit(F-150 pickup truck)

In addition to fire and EMS services, the department also offers many other services and programs to benefit Green Township residents. The first program offered by the department is the car seat inspection program. Green Township Fire & EMS has certified Car Seat Technicians who attend regular classes through Cincinnati Children's Hospital and the American Automobile Association. These checks involve parents bringing in their car seats to inspect a seat to ensure proper installation. These inspections, which can take 30-45 minutes, have become a welcome benefit to both new and experienced parents. In addition, these checks provide peace of mind that their children will be protected in an unfortunate automobile accident.

Another popular service the Green Township Fire & EMS department provides is the Community Heartsaver CPR program. These CPR classes are offered to people living or working in Green Township and are free of charge. These classes generally cover bystander CPR for adults, children, and infants, in addition to Automated External Defibrillator(AED) and choking training. CPR classes are offered at Station 54 on Bridgetown Road usually once a month.

One of the department's most vital safety programs is its smoke detector program. The Green Township Fire & EMS Department assists residents unable to install battery-operated smoke detectors. The department also assists residents in changing batteries in smoke detectors if assistance is needed. This program has been one of the longest-running outreach programs, returning to the MVFD days of fire protection and prevention.

The Green Township Fire & EMS department provides many other outreach programs. For example, the Medic Bike Team program offers first aid and emergency medical care at significant public events in Green Township. This team is specially trained to operate bikes in crowded or difficult locations. The bikes are outfitted with medical equipment specially designed for this use, which includes small defibrillators, oxygen bottles, and other supplies for people in need in more difficult-to-access locations. The Community Emergency Response Team or CERT training program instructs participants from the community to become experts in assisting responders in a major emergency, such as a tornado, earthquake, flooding, or other potentially significant catastrophes, such as a lengthy power outage affecting the township.

Finally, one of the most effective forms of outreach to residents is the department's demonstrations to the schools and groups in the Green Township community. The Green Township,

Fire & EMS Department will also provide tours of their stations to community groups or individuals. The department has developed many presentations for these tours, including programs for young children, which entails using 911 and stop-drop-and-roll education; pre-teen and teen programs which involve what to do when an ambulance arrives as well as merit badge programs for scouting groups; and finally adult programs which see demonstrations of equipment and education on how the fire and EMS department operates. The Green Township Fire & EMS will also visit neighborhood parties, perform equipment demonstrations, and conduct meet and greets. These demonstrations and programs allow the department to engage with the township's residents in a non-emergency setting and give the public insight into the inner workings of how the modern fire and EMS operates.

Many other changes occurred in the 21st century in Green Township, including a gradual population increase every ten years on the US Census. With the 2020 census, Green Township showed well over 60,000 residents. Despite a growing population and the demand it places on public services, Green Township Fire & EMS has continued to serve the people with distinction, receiving the American Heart Association Mission Lifeline-EMS Gold Plus Award for Cardiac Care for over six years. This award shows how the department goes above and beyond in its care and service provided to the township.

The department has also seen a significant loss of part-time employees due to a hyper-competitive job market in the 21st century. The department, being ever vigilant of the demands it faces daily for staffing, has added 15 full-time staff to keep up with the loss of part-time employees. The loss of part-time employees is a big concern in both the State of Ohio and Hamilton County in the latter half of the 2010s and early 2020s. Two safety services tax levies passed in 2014 and 2022 have significantly helped the department with the loss of these part-time employees by providing additional money to the department. This enables hiring more full-time employees to improve the coverage of shifts. The Fire and EMS Department is cautious about how they spend the tax levy, always mindful of the trust the public and taxpayers give the department.

Why the red truck???

Green Township Fire & EMS ran into a unique situation in 2019. The department relies heavily on a spare apparatus to fill in when any vehicle in its fleet is in need of maintenance. It was discovered that the spare apparatus at the time, a 1999 Sutphen Pumper, has an unsafe rust condition affectin the vehicles main frame. The cost to fix the much-needed vehicle was estimated at well over $60,000, and the repairs might take over three months. At the same time, the Anderson Township Fire Department was selling a used pumper for $40,000. The department purchased this used pumper from Anderson Township, a 2002 Central States Pumper at a better price than repairing the old vehicle, which could be put into service two weeks after purchase. The only issue was that the pumper was red, unlike all Green Township Fire & EMS apparatus, which are white. The cost was too high to repaint the apparatus white, so the red color stayed.

Many Green Township residents give the pumper puzzled looks when it drives by on township roads. This is because since 1954, going back to the MVFD, the color schemes for the vehicles have been white. The Mack chief at the time felt the department vehicles needed more visibility during dark hours on the township roads, so white has been the standard, which has been carried over into the Green Township Fire & EMS.

A point of pride from the 21st century fire and EMS department comes from the 9/11 memorial dedicated September 11, 2013, in front of the Green Township Administration complex. The monument consists of a piece of steel recovered from the World Trade Center. The 12-foot steel beam was recovered from Ground Zero and was donated to Green Township by the Port Authority of New York and New Jersey. The work began with the Green Township Administration, Green Township Fire & EMS, and private citizens who worked with the Port Authority of New York and New Jersey to bring the steel to Green Township. In addition, several Green Township Firefighters made the journey to the New York area to accompany the steel to Green Township. The memorial is a testament to the bravery and dedication of the rescue personnel who worked hard to recover as many individuals as they could after the 9/11 attacks and the dedication of all rescue personnel in the Green Township area. This monument is open for all to see and contemplate the gravity of the sacrifice of the men and women who lost their lives on 9/11.

In 2022, The Green Township Fire & EMS mission statement pledges that the department will "successfully deliver professional service to the community through education, prevention, and response while embracing department values(compassion, respect, and integrity)." This vision harkens to the MVFD motto: "We serve to save." Green Township residents have been fortunate to have two organizations dedicated to saving the property of the township residents and protecting their lives.

Green Township Trustee Tony Rosiello(center), previous Green Township Police Chief Bart West(left), and previous Green Township Fire & EMS Chief Doug Witsken by the new 9/11 Memorial at the Green Township Administration Building. Several Firefighters from Green Township Fire & EMS accompanied the piece of steel, which was recovered from the Twin Towers in New York City. (Photo courtesy Green Township Fire & EMS)

A Quint Fire Truck is housed at Station 53 on Harrison Avenue. This unit shares space with an ambulance, the spare pumper, as well as the command staff of the fire department. (Photo courtesy Green Township Fire & EMS)

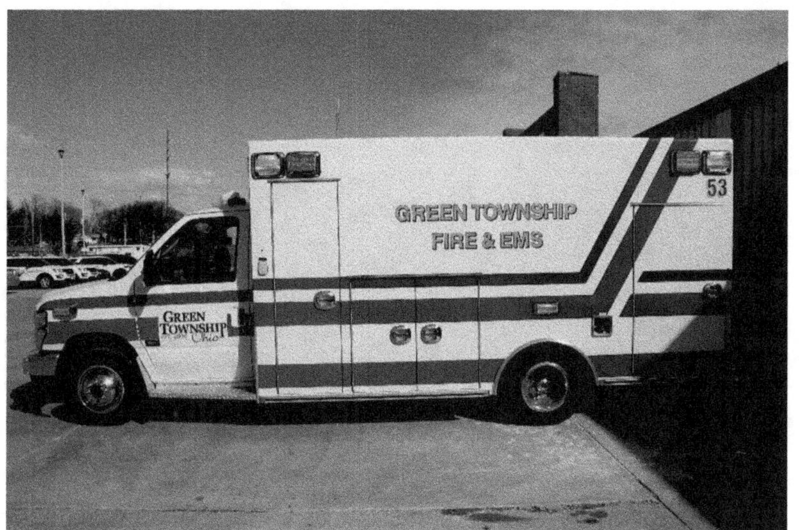

The ambulance housed at Station 53 on Harrison Avenue. This vehicle shares space with the Quint, the spare pumper, and the department's command staff. (Photo courtesy Green Township Fire & EMS)

This red pumper is housed at Station 53 on Harrison Avenue in Dent. It is the "spare" fire engine for the department, and its primary function is to fill in for other fire apparatus when maintenance is performed on those vehicles. (Photo courtesy Green Township Fire & EMS)

This pumper is housed at Station 54 on Bridgetown Road, along with an ambulance and a John Deere Gator utility vehicle for use at special events. (Photo courtesy Green Township Fire & EMS)

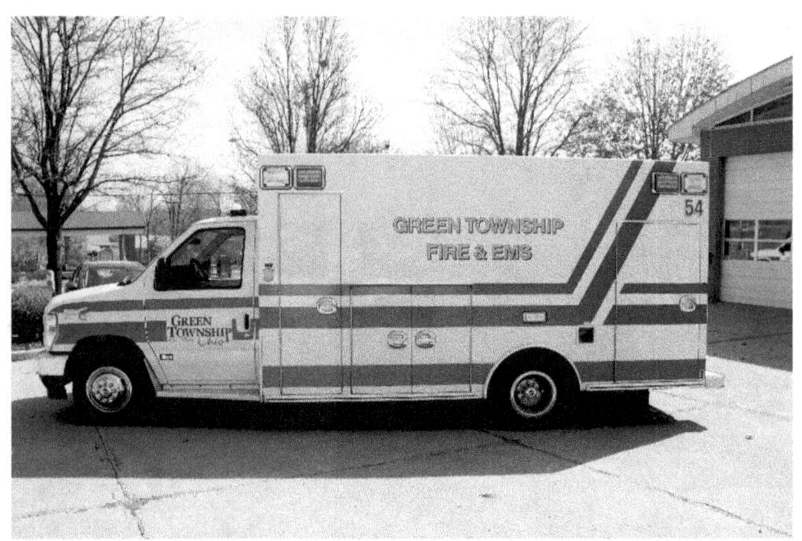

This ambulance is housed at Station 54 on Bridgetown Road, along with a pumper and John Deere Gator utility vehicle. (Photo courtesy Green Township Fire & EMS)

This John Deere Gator utility vehicle was donated to Green Township Fire & EMS by Mack Fire Inc. through their fundraising activities. This is housed at Station 54 on Bridgetown Road and is used during special events like festivals or when access for larger vehicles is difficult. (Photo courtesy Green Township Fire & EMS)

This pumper is housed at Station #55 on West Fork Road at Audro Drive. This station also houses an ambulance and fire investigation truck. (Photo courtesy Green Township Fire & EMS)

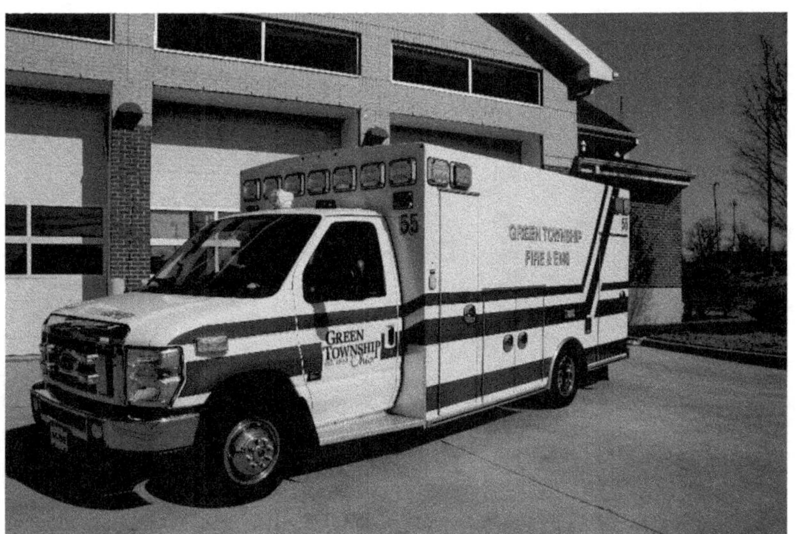

This ambulance is housed at Station 55 on West Fork Road at Audro Drive, along with a pumper engine. This serves Monfort Heights and White Oak in Green Township. (Photo courtesy Green Township Fire & EMS)

This pumper is housed at Station 107 on Sylved Road in the Covedale neighborhood of southern Green Township. An ambulance is housed here as well. (Photo courtesy Green Township Fire & EMS)

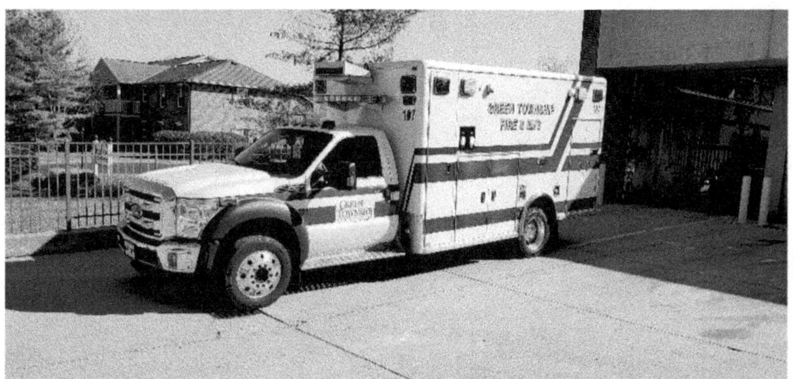

This ambulance is housed at Station 107 on Sylved Road near Muddy Creek Road. This vehicle shares space with a pumper and serves the Covedale neighborhood of southern Green Township. (Photo courtesy Green Township Fire & EMS)

Appendix 1

List of Mack Volunteer Fire Department Members, Green Township Fire & EMS Members, MVFD Ladies Auxiliary, and MVFD Dispatchers

Please Note: Mack Fire Inc. and Green Township Fire & EMS attempted to include every name associated with the Mack Volunteer Fire Department, Ladies Auxiliary, Volunteer Dispatchers, and Green Township Fire & EMS from its first decades of existence to the switchover to an arm of Green Township government to the end of 2022. Unfortunately, not all names may be included due to the condition of some records or inaccurate records. For any other information, including ranks, firehouse, and any additional information regarding a particular member and their service, contact Mack Fire Inc through www.mackfire.org or Green Township Fire & EMS. All information, including spelling, is believed to be accurate as of publication

Abbitello, Tyler
Abel, Joe
Adams, Ray
Adams, Sharon
Adamson, Prescott
Adamson, Sherman
Adkinson, Orville
Adkinson, Thelma
Adkinson, Wilbert
Ahlers, Betty
Ahlers, Heinz
Ahlers, Mary
Ahlers, Rolf
Aisenbrey, Don
Aisenbrey, John
Aisenbrey, Judy
Albertz, Dan
Alexander, Steven

Allgeir, Ed
Allstatter, Karl
Arand Jr., William
Arend, Tom
Arends, Angela
Arlington, John
Atkinson, Mary
Atkinson, Thelma
Atkinson, Wilber (Red)
Auberger, Len
Auel, Al
Axt, Paul
Baer, William
Baker, Doug
Baker, Joe
Baker, Samuel
Ball, Frank
Ball, Robert
Ballachino, Frank
Bamberger, Delores
Bamberger, James
Barnes, William
Barnharst, Harold
Barry, Jack
Barvancik, Joseph
Bastian, Robert
Bauer, John
Bauer, Marjie
Baum, Tony
Bauman, Adam
Bauman, Jeff
Baumer, Joel
Baumgartner, John
Bavaro, Scott
Bayer, Jeffrey
Beal, Charles
Beckemeyer, John
Becker, Arlene
Becker,Willard
Beckmann, Barb
Beiler, Cindy
Beischel, Jim
Bell, Richard
Bell, Thomas
Bell,Tony
Bender, Doris
Bender, Eugene
Bender, Jeanette
Bender, Ralph
Bengal, Mike
Benken, David
Benkert, Thomas
Bennett,Claude
Beraurer, Clem
Bergman, Elliot
Bering, James
Berling, Michael
Berning, Jim
Berning, Mary Ellen
Black, Harold
Blakely, Foster
Bleh, Michael
Blum, Raymond
Blum, Rudolf
Boeckermann, Frank
Boeckermann, Michael
Boggs, Arlis
Bohning, John

Bollinger, Alfred
Bollinger,Gill
Bolser, Jeremy
Bootes, M.
Booth Jr., James
Bosken, Jay
Bosse, Joshua
Bouchonnet, Joe
Bouchonnet, Juliette
Boyde, Harry
Boyle, Allen
Brandes, Ralph
Branigan, Michael
Braun, Andrew
Braun, Bob
Braun, Kevin
Braun, Sarah
Bredwell, Larry
Brehm, Justin
Brent, Landen
Brewer, Darrell
Brielmaier, Rose
Briemaier,William
Brockhoff, Bob
Brockhoff, Dale
Brockhoff, Jason
Brockhoff, Judy
Brockhoff, Terry
Brockman, Mary Ann
Brogan, Ethan
Brogan, Mike
Brooks, Amy
Bross, Bill
Bross, Larry
Brown, Charles
Brown, Christopher (CJ)
Brown, Dennis
Brown, Morton
Broz, Linda
Brubaker, Mike
Brunsman, Jeffrey
Bryant, David
Bucher, Brian
Buckart, J.W
Burbrink, Brian
Burke, James
Burkhardt, Jake
Buse, Ted
Butscha, Tom
Cafazzo, Ben
Cafazzo, Elaine
Camp, David
Campbell, Tom
Campbell,UNKNOWN
Carle Jr, Ralph
Carle Sr, Ralph
Carle, Alvin
Carle, Edwina
Carmack, Deborah
Carmack, Tom
Carpenter, Tanner
Carr, Kasey
Carraher, Kevin
Carraher, Nicholas
Case, Gary
Case, Ken
Cavanaugh, Bob

Chastang, David
Chastang, Dennis
Chastang, Diane
Chastang, James
Chastang, Linda
Chastang, Scott
Chastang, Tim
Chetwood, Blaine
Childs, Dan
Childs, Mike
Chinn, Pauline
Chinn, Shirley
Christman, Gloria
Christman, John
Christo, Ken
Claytor, Steve
Clemends, Larry
Clemends, Roseanne
Clements Jr., Edward
Clements Sr., Edward
Connelly, Mike
Conners, William
Cook, Joshua
Cooke, Ed
Corcoran, Eric
Crackel, Jack
Crawford, Ed
Creech, Charles
Creech, Evelyn
Creeden, Edward
Creighton, Craig
Crone, Joshua
Crone, Robert
Daniels, Ben
Darby, Bill
Darst, Blair
Davis, Jason
Davis, Jeff
Davis, Larry
Dawson, Jeffrey
Day, Cathy
Day, Joe
Dektas, Diane
Dellerman, Charles
Dellerman, Louise
Dennert, Ralph
Detzel, Edward
Dickman, Bill
Dickman, Edith
Diehl, Michael
Diehl, Steve
Diem, Otto
Dietz, Mary
Dietz, Thomas
Dimuzio, Mike
Discepoli, Michael
Disser, David
Doherty, Robert
Donahue, Michael
Donisi, Dominic
Donisi, Phyllis
Donohue, Edward
Donohue, Mike
Donohue, Sharon
Dooley, Joyce
Dorenkemper, Ginny
Dorenkemper, Joe
Douglas, Michael

Dove, Rick
Downie, James
Draise, Mike
Dreier, Dan
Dreiss, Joe
Dreyer, Janet
Driskell, Dave
Driskell, Stella
Duell, Laverne
Duell, Ray
Dufford, James
Duffy,Kevin
Duke, James
Duke, Nathan
Eaves, Jason
Eckhoff, Jason
Eckhoff, Jim
Edwards, Jason
Edwards, Layton
Eichorn, Carl
Eisenacher, Ann
Eisenacher, David
Eisenacker, George
Eisenecher, Bob
Eisenecher, Ron
Elkins Jr., Ray
Ellert, Randy
Elliott, Ray
Elsbernd, Sandy
Elsbernd, Thomas
Enderle, Louis
Enderle-Montoya, Madelyn
Engelbrink, Marie
Engelbrink, R.
Engelhart, Paul (Line of duty death 1963)
Eninger, Chris
Enswinger, Phil
Ernst, Walter
Evans, Charles
Evans, Sharon
Faetly, Harold
Faulhaber, Robert
Fenner, Roman
Filbert, Dave
Filbert, Dot
Fiorini, George
Fischer, Barb
Fischer, Ed
Fisher, Barbara
Fisher, Bob
Fisher, Virginia
Flach, Robert
Flagler, Matt
Fledderman, Bill
Fletterman, Jim
Flick, Zachary
Fliehman, Kevin
Flynn, Chrissy
Fogel, Mark
Forman, Todd
Forster, Craig
Fox, Brian
Fox, Rick
Fox, Sylvia
Fox, Tom
Foy, William

Frank, Donald
Frey, Bill
Frey, Dave
Frey, Dottie
Frey, Joe
Frey, John
Frey, Rick
Frondorf, Bert
Frondorf, Edward
Frondorf, Gus
Frondorf, Henry
Frondorf, Linda
Frondorf, Ray
Frost, John
Fulton, Bill
Gallagher, Daniel
Galligan, Dan
Garbon, Paul
Garvey, Kevin
Gaston, Louretta
Gaston, Terry
Gaub, William
Gaynor, Marjorie
Gaynor, Mark
Gaynor, Ned
Gaynor, Tom
Gehring, Nicholas
Geier, Harry
Geiger, Lou
Geiger, Robert
Geiser, Jason
Gemereth, Chuck
Gemmell Jr., Ray
Gemmell Sr., Ray
Gemmell, Chris
Gemmell, Dave
Gemmell, Nikolas
Gemmell, Pam
Gemmell, Rose
Gibeau, George
Gibeau, June
Gibson, Charles
Ginn, Carol
Ginn, Rick
Glaeser, Carol
Glaeser,(Unknown)
Glascock, Jerry
Gnoose, Barbra
Gnoose, Jerry
Goddard, William
Godfrey, Christopher
Goetz, Stephen
Goldschmidt, Scott
Gooden, Jerome
Grarat, George
Greek, Steve
Gresham, Lee
Groshardt, George
Grubbs, Matt
Gruener, Jack
Gruener, Sally
Guenthner, Joyce
Gunn, Alexander
Gunn, Patrick
Gunn, Trevor
Hafertepen, Ed
Hafertepen, Joyce
Hall, Pete

Hallendorf, Carl
Hamm, Nicholas
Handley, Christopher
Handley, Patrick
Hannekamp, Glen
Harden, Brad
Hardiman, John
Harley, Gary
Harley, Todd
Harris, David
Hass, Andy
Hass, Ray
Hastie, Charles
Hastie, Chick
Hathaway, John
Hattendorf, Carl
Hattendorf, Eleanor
Hattendorf, Gail
Hattendorf, Ross
Haus, Jim
Haverland, James
Hay, John
Heekin, Christopher
Heidi, Kristi
Hein, Dick
Hein, Don
Hein, Gladys
Hein, Helen
Hein, Paul
Heintz, Jeffrey
Heithaus, Leo
Heitker, William
Helmes, Sydney
Henke, Ken
Henricks, Herman
Herbert, Clarence
Herbert, Donald
Herbert, Forrest (Fats)
Herbert, Helen
Herbert, Inez
Herbert, John
Herbert, Mike
Herzog, Richard
Hettesheimer, Richard
Hetzel, Mark
High, John
Hildebrand, Dan
Hildebrand, Mark
Hildebrand, Steve
Hildebrand, Sue
Hill, Jeanette
Hill, R.
Hillebrand, Mark
Hilton, Ronald
Hilton, Walter
Hinds, Gavin
Hinson, Scott
Hodapp, Bryce
Hoggins, Fred
Hoh, Maryann
Hoh, Rick
Hollmeyer, Bev
Hollmeyer, Ray
Hollmeyer, Rose
Holmstrom, Dorothy
Holmstrom, Paul
Honnert, Joe
Hoog, Carl

Hoog, Patricia
Horne, (Unknown)
Horne, Kathy
Horning, Laura
Horning, Raymond
Hosick, Robert
Hubbertz, John
Huber, Jim
Huber, Karol
Huber, Rick
Huff, Novie
Hughes, Clarence
Hughes, Keith
Hughes, Thelma
Hull, Alfred (Pete)
Hull, Georgiana
Hull, Jerry
Hull, Joann
Hull, Thomas
Hummeldorf, Brian
Hummeldorf, Elaine
Hummeldorf, Kevin
Humphrey, Doug
Hurlburt, Omer
Hustedt, Buddy
Hustedt, Carol
Huth, Tom
Ihle, Andy
Inderhees, Ann
Inderhees, Ken
James, Howard
Jeffries, Emily
Jennings, David
Jobst, J.
Jodice, Cary
Jorg, Janet
Jorg, Rick
Joseph, Michael
Juengling, Gary
Juengling, Laverne
Juengling, Nancy
Juengling, Tony
Jung, David
Kain, Linda
Kain, Steve
Kaiser, Andy
Kaiser, Barbara
Kallendorf, Bob
Kallendorf, Kathy
Kamuf, Betty
Kamuf, Bonnie
Kamuf, Don
Kappa, Michael
Kappen, Jeff
Kavanaugh, Robert
Keck, Chick
Keck, Lorain
Keene, Tim
Keeton, Tim
Kegley, Brian
Keil, Nicholas
Kelley, Mike
Kercheval, Kurt
Kercheval, Scott
Kern, Herb
Kern, Joann
Keylor, David
Kiefer, Blaine

Kiefer, Tom
King, Lisa
Kinross, Ron
Kirchner, Jeanette
Kirchner, Whitey
Kirry, Eugene
Kist, Richard
Kitchen, Robert
Klaene, Mark
Klausing, Matthew
Klayer, Don
Klayer, Kathy
Kluener, Barry
Kluener, Bob
Kluener, Don
Kluener, Michael
Kluener, Steve
Klug, Christopher
Knapp, Andrew
Knapp, Dale
Knapp, Leslie
Knorr, Allen
Knorr, Wanda
Koch, Edward
Korb, Andrew
Korb, Tom
Kotte, Thomas
Kramer, Bill
Kramer, Jack
Krass, Ronald
Krebs, Ralph
Kreft, (Unknown)
Kreft, Ann
Kreimer, Earl
Kreimer, Kathy
Kreimer, Martha
Krekler, Jeanette
Kroeger, Matthew
Kruesling, Jim
Krutzcamp, Jeff
Kuchenmeister, Dan
Kulback, Ida
Kulback, Manuel
Laake, Marc
Lameier, Robert
Lammers, Jeff
Lane, Linda
Lange, Sean
Langhorst, Gill
Langhorst, Jeanette
Lanter, Mike
Lauderback, Gary
Lautz, Suzanne
Leach, Andre
Leahy, Charles
Lecture, Tom
Ledford, James
Lehman, Irene
Lehman, Mel
Lehman, Robert
Leibel, Bubbles
Leibel, Jeanette
Leibel, Norb
Lemmink, Martin
Leone, Anthony
Leppert, Tylery
Leurs, Ed
Lewallen, Kevin

Leytze , Keith
Leytze, Mark
Lietemeyer, Ray
Lifer, Chad
Lingers, Joseph
Lingers, Lorainne
Link, Brian
Link, Robert
Linne, Brandon
Lintz, Dan
Lipp, Bill
Lippay, Norb
Lipps, Cal
Lipps, Lucille
Lohrmans, Ed
Lorton, Ellie
Lotz, Mike
Louden, Diane
Louden, Shelby
Louderback, Anthony
Louderback, Gary
Louis, Theodore
Lucus, Cliff
Ludmann, Stephen
Ludwig, Larry
Ludwig, Steve
Luning, Jacob
Lupp, Dave
Lustenberger, Michael
Luttrell, Ken
Lutz, James
Mahan, Kevin
Mahan, Kurt
Mainwaring, David
Makstaller, Joe
Maloney, Steve
Mangold, Walter
Mara, Tom
Marshal, Dean
Marshal, George
Marshall, Dean
Martin, Larry
Martin, Ronald
Martini, Dean
Masson, Gary
Masson, Kyle
Masters, John
Mathews, Jerry
Matthews, Carol
Matthews, Gerald
Matthey, Dale
Matthey, Joyce
Maxwell, Gerald
Maxwell, Lois
May, Ben
May, Shawn
McCarren, Ed
McCarthy, C.
McCormick, James
McCreadie, Randy
McDonald, Kory
McElroy, Joe
McElvain, Larwence
McFarland, Dennis
McKeehan, Lisa
McManus, Michael
McSorley, James
McWilliams, Brendan

Meese, Steve
Meisel, Max
Menke, Dave
Menke, Jim
Merschback, Gary
Metz, Gladys
Metz, Robert
Metzger, John
Meyer, Ben
Meyer, Charles
Meyer, Cody
Meyer, Ed
Meyer, George
Meyer, John
Meyer, Paul
Meyer, Pauline
Meyer, Ronald
Meyer, Todd
Meyer, Vince
Meyers, Frank
Meyers, Louis
Meyers, Whitey
Milazzo, William
Miles, Bob
Miles, Mike
Miles, Sandra
Miller, Paul
Miller, Ron
Minges, Doctor Ted
Minning, Tom
Misch, Donna
Misch, Wayne
Mischell, Charles
Mischell, Wayne
Mitchell, John
Moelder, Leo
Mohr, Andy
Mohr, Gary
Mohr, Nancy
Moody, Justin
Mooney, Darren
Moore, Arlene
Moore, Brian
Moore, Frank
Moore, Jesse
Morgan, Darlene
Morgan, Hunter
Morgan, Robert
Morris, Walter
Morton, Robert
Mueller, Stan
Mueller, Toddy
Mullins, Mike
Muntz, Otto
Murdock, Donald
Murphy, John
Murphy, Michael
Murphy, Mike
Murphy, Zachary
Myers, Michael
Myers, Shaun
Myers, Steve
Myers, Todd
Nathenson, Melvin
Nelson, Frank
Neu, Bill
Neyer, Ben
Nichols, Charles

Nicodemus, Guthrie
Nie, (Unknown)
Nie, Jeanette
Nie, Mike
Niehiesel, Bill
Nieman, Gary
Nieman, Henrietta
Nieman, Jerry
Niemer, Matthew
Niemeyer, William
Nienaber, Michael
Niesen, Tom
Nix, Martha
Nix, Wilson
Noble, Betty
Noble, Jerry
Nolte, Carl
Nolte, Jeanette
Nolte, Roger
Obermeyer, Jeff
O'Brien, Adam
Oehler, Dorothy
Oehler, Robert
Oevermeyer, Marty
Ohe, Bruce
Osterkamp, Dan
Osterkamp, Don
Osterkamp, Rita
Ott, Lou
Overbeck,Ken
Overberg, Steve
Pagliaro, Ethan
Parker, Andrew
Parrett, Rodney
Patterson, Donald
Paulinelli, Roger
Payne, Jason
Payne, Justin
Pennekamp, Ryan
Perkins, Harvey
Perkins, Larry
Perkins, Lee
Peters, Jack
Peters, Jerry
Peters, John
Peters, Joseph
Peters, Lynn
Peters, Tom
Pfaff, Betty
Pfaff, Harvey
Pflanger, Steve
Pflanzer, Jack
Pflanzer, Viola
Phillips, Cliff
Phillips, Evelyn
Phillips, Joe
Phillips, John
Pichiney, James
Pickens Jr., Cliff
Pickens, Cliff
Pickens, Grace
Pickering, Ryan
Pies, Chris
Pies, Edward
Pio, Brian
Pizzato, Antonia
Pizzuto, Tony
Poehner, Jerry

Pollard, Robert
Posega, Chris
Potter, Steve
Powell, Jack
Preece, Greg
Pritchard, Ben
Prock, James
Pursifull, Mary Jo
Pursifull, Mike
Putthoff, Fred
Puttoff, Carol
Queenan, Robert ("Rusty")
Rack, Jeff
Rack, Jerry
Rack, Jim
Raellinger, Steve
Raible, Brett
Raling, Walter
Ralphy, John
Rapking, Juanita
Rapking, William
Raterman, John
Rauh Jr., Stan
Rauh, Dan
Rauh, Stan
Rebold, Peter
Rechin, Clarence
Redmond, Hal
Reeves, Randall
Reinert, Austin
Reitzes, Carol
Rettig, Diane
Rettig, Joseph
Rhodes, Dick
Rhodes, Gert
Rhodes, Jane
Rhodes, Janet
Rhodes, Kevin
Rielage, Tom
Riessig, Ferd
Riga, Jim
Rinear, Jonah
Robb, Jill
Robb, Richard
Roberto, Dale
Roberto, Marie
Rodriquez, Amy
Roehrig, Joe
Roesel, Zack
Rosenacker, Clarence
Rosenacker, Frank
Rosenacker, Joseph
Rothenbush, Clarence
Rothenbush, Shirley
Rottmueller, Dan
Rottmueller, Frank
Rottmueller, Mary Jo
Roy, Michelle
Ruberg, Rex
Ruberg, Roger
Ruberg, Ross
Ruberg, Russ
Ruberg, Ruth
Ruberg, Ryan
Ruberry Jr., William
Ruehl, (Unknown)
Ruehl, Mathilda

Ruehlman, Butch
Ruehlman, Della
Ruehlman, Harry
Ruehlman, Robert
Ruepert, Dan
Russo, Mark
Rutenschroer, James
Rutenscroher, Pat
Ruther, Leo
Ruttig, Joe
Rutz, Herschel
Ruwe, Chris
Ruwe, Gene
Ryan, Ed
Ryan, Sandy
Sabers, Joseph
Sabers, William
Sandy, (Unknown)
Sanker, Darren
Sanker, David
Santiago, Gretchen
Sawyer, George
Sayne Jr., John
Sayne Sr., John
Sayne, Elaine
Sayne, Gary
Sayne, Gerry
Schaefer, Jeffrey
Schaefer, Phyllis
Schaeperklaus, Rae
Schafer, Douglas
Schalk, Howard
Schalk, Rosella
Scheffel, Wilbert
Scheider, Doug
Schell ,Bill
Schell, Norma
Scherer, Michael
Schiffmeyer Jr., Harry
Schiffmeyer Sr., Harry
Schlensker, Don
Schlensker, Joan
Schlensker, Joan
Schlensker, Ron
Schloemer, Tom
Schloss, Dot
Schloss, Laura
Schloss, Marty
Schmidt, Edward
Schmidt, Steve
Schmithorst, Matthew
Schmitt Jr., Franklin
Schmitt, William
Schneeberger, Paul
Schneider, Cliff
Schneider, Doug
Schneider, Greg
Schneider, Greg
Schotte, Harold
Schrader, Carl
Schrader, Olga
Schrage, Josh
Schrand, Ken
Schrand, Ken
Schrantz, (Unknown)
Schrantz, Rita
Schroeder, Myrl
Schroeder, Nelson

Schroer, Andy
Schrout, Bob
Schulte, Albert
Schulte, Gayle
Schulte, Hub
Schulte, Melva
Schutte, Harold
Schwarz, Ryan
Schwoeppe, Cecilia
Schwoeppe, George
Schwoeppe, George
Scott, Jim
Sears, Robert
Seiler, Jeff
Sellers, Al
Senft, Steve
Seng, Carl
Seng, Pat
Seng, Roger
Seng, Ruth
Seurkamp, Bill
Seurkamp, Joan
Sexton, Earl
Seyfried, Ron
Seymour, Laurence
Sherron, Mike
Shires, Kyle
Shrout, Robert
Siegel, Don
Simon, Steve
Skidmore, Charles
Smith Jr., Al
Smith Sr., Al
Smith, Coy
Smith, Fred
Smith, Gary
Smith, Harry
Smith, Janet
Smith, June
Smith, Kevin
Smith, Lillian
Smith, Michael
Smith, Ryan
Smith, Tom
Smith, Val
Smith, William
Smith, Zachary
Snodgrass, Jacob
Snow, James
Soaper, Jack
Souders, Curtis
Souders, Scott
Southard, Terry
Spade, Bill
Spears, Joe
Sper, John
Spindler, Gordon
Stahmer, Don
Stahmer, Judy
Stall, Dick
Stall, Ginny
Stange, Larry
Stanton, Edward
Stauffer, Andrew
Stautberg, William
Steel, Milton
Steinmann, Charles
Steinmann, Edward

Steinmann, Myrtle
Stenger, Jim
Stenger, Nick
Stevens, Jack
Stiehl, M.
Stigler, Dave
Stiles, Dave
Stock, Christopher
Stortz, Chris
Stout, David
Street, Rob
Stroschen, Walter
Stroschen, William
Sucietto, John
Suder, Mike
Sudhoff, Lester
Sudhoff, Muriel
Sue Schloss
Sullender, Eric
Sunderhaus, Jim
Sutter, Terry
Sutton, Frank
Sutton, Shawn
Swadener, Dave
Swart, Dorothea
Swart, Henry
Swart, Mary
Swarts, George
Sweeney, Bob
Sweeney, Carol
Sweeney, Chris
Sweeney, Emmett
Sweeney, Kathleen
Sweeney, Lillian
Sweeney, Tom
Sweet, Jeff
Szurlinski, Tom
Tabler, Ben
Tate, Terry
Tate, Tim
Tenoever,William
Tepe, William
Theiring, Fred
Thesing, Gregory
Theurer, Gary
Theurer, Mark
Theurer, Mary
Theuring, (Unknown)
Theuring, Dorothy
Thiessen, Brian
Thinnes, Carol
Thinnes, Danny
Thinnes, Dutch
Thinnes, Howard
Thinnes, Joe
Thomas, Edward
Thomas, Judy
Thomas, Marge
Thompson, James
Thorp, Barbara
Thorp, Betty
Thorp, Mike
Tierney, Betty
Tierney, Tom
Tigges, Bernard
Tilford, Ron
Tilley, Sean
Timmers, Terry

Tobergta, James
Tobergta, Jean
Totten, Bill
Totten, Marian
Trame, Tim
Triplett, Clarence
Troescher, John
Truitt, Austin
Truitt, Betty
Truitt, Jesse
Tvrdy, Joe
Ulrich, Paul
Ultsch, Bill
Valentino, Vince
VandeRyt, Richard
Vanselow, Bill
Vanselow, Ernie
Vanselow, Virginia ("Ginger")
Vaske, Ken
Veldhaus, James
Veldhaus, Joshua
Verdin, Jamison
Vetter, William
Viox, Bob
Voekel, Thomas
Vollmer, George
Volz, John
Von Walden, Lou
Vosseberg, Erna
Vosseberg, Frank
Vosseberg, Paul
Vultagio, Mike
Wagner, Elmer
Wagner, Kevin
Wagner, Mark
Wagner, Tom
Waldorf, Dwight
Waldorf, Mary Lou
Waldorf, Peggy
Waldorf, Wally
Waldsmith, Ed
Walker, Dennis
Walker, Georgiana
Walker, James
Waller, Robert
Walsh, Walter
Walters, Jeffrey
Walters, Mark
Washington, Mike
Wasserman, Bubbles
Wasserman, Stan
Webber, Anita
Weber, Doug
Weber, Ken
Weber, Rick
Weber, Vernon
Weberding, Doug
Weberding, Eric
Weghorst, Carl
Weghorst, Mary Lou
Weichert, Dennis
Weidner, Delores
Weidner, Ronald
Weidner, Sheila
Weil, Eric
Weingartner, Anthony
Weissmann, Michael

Weitzel Sr., Robert
Weitzel, Cle
Weitzel, David
Weitzel, Doug
Weitzel, Edith
Weitzel, Robert
Weitzel, Robert
Weitzel, Rose
Welge, Hal
Welge, Helen
Welge, Judy
Wells, Michael
Wenger, Phil
Wengert, Art
Wentzel, Audrey
Wentzel, Steve
Werk, Louis
Werle, Flora
Werle, Ralph
Wernke, Mike
Wessels, Art
Wessels, Florence
Westlund, George ("Bud")
White, Gary
Whittington, Neil
Wied, Mark
Wieseman, Willard
Wiesner, William
Wilburn, Conner
Wiley, Roy
Wilhelm, Gary
Willenbrink, Barbara
Willenbrink, George
Williams, Jeffrey
Williams, Rich
Williams, Ronald
Williamson, Mike
Willis, Bob
Willis, Cecil
Wilson, Andrew
Wilson, Chris
Wilson, Cy
Wilson, James
Wilson, Jeff
Wilson, Jeff
Wilson, Melissa
Wilson, Vernon
Wilz, Jim
Wilz, Marty
Wilz, Mike
Wisinell, Bob
Wisinell, Sue
Wissemeier, Todd
Witsken, Douglas
Witsken, Scott
Wittekind, Ron
Wohlfrom, Robert
Wolf, Joe
Woods, Dale
Wooley, J.
Wortman, Angela
Wortman, Ed
Wortman, Rita
Wright, Matthew
Wuebbling, Joshua
Wullenweber, Wilber
Wunder, Doug

Wurtz, Ed
Wyatt, Don
Wyder, Samuel
Wysong, Les
Yeazel, Duane
Yeazel, Lillie May
Young, Dave
Yuellig, Frank
Zaeske, Charles
Zaeske, Samuel
Zaeske, Tom
Zang, Arlene
Zang, Don
Zeek, Joe
Zeek, Robert
Zehnder, Don
Ziegler, Derek
Zorb, Bud
Zorick, George (Line of duty death 1977)

Appendix 2
Mack Volunteer Fire Department Chiefs

Ed Luhrman(Honorary) 1944-1946
Ed Steinman, 1947
Robert Metz, 1947-1958
Joseph Lingers, 1958-1963
Stan Mueller, 1963-1966
Donald Schlensker, 1966-1974
Robert Weitzel, 1974-1978
Hal Welge, 1979

Appendix 3
Green Township Fire & EMS Chiefs

Robert Weitzel, 1980-2005
Doug Witsken, 2005-2017
Scott Souders, 2017-Present

Appendix 4
Mack Fire Incorporated Presidents

Dick Stall, 1983-1984
Ed Wortman, 1985-1986
Forest Herbert, 1987-1990
Don Schlensker, 1991-1992
Rich Hoh, 1993-1996
Don Kamuf, 1997-1998
Bob Sears, 1999-2002
Carl Weghorst, 2003-2006
Mike Pursifull, 2007-2010
Frank Hoh, 2011-2016
Ed Wortman, 2017-2018
Dennis Chastang, 2019 to Present

Appendix 5
Mack Volunteer Fire Department Rolling Stock, 1944 through 1983

This list shows the vehicles the Mack Volunteer Fire Department acquired from 1947 to 1983. Some of the vehicles were purchased through fundraisers, and some from gifts. This information includes the year the vehicle was made, the cost, if known, the make of the vehicle, and any description. Unfortunately, some information is missing due to the age and condition of the records.

Year	Cost	Make	Gas or Diesel	Description
1947	$1,934	Federal	Gas	1 ½ Ton Pumper, From Battle Creek Michigan
1930 Era	Gift	Dodge	Gas	Converted Old Civil Defense Pumper
1930 Era	Gift	Sterling	Gas	Army Air Corp. Runway Pumper (Old Mo)
1953		GMC	Gas	Panel Van Ambulance, First Owned by Dept.
1954		GMC	Gas	American Fire Apparatus 500 GPM Pumper
1956		GMC	Gas	American Fire Apparatus 500 GPM Pumper
1957		GMC	Gas	American Fire Apparatus 500 GPM Pumper

1959		Cadillac	Gas	Hess/Eisenhart Ambulance
1961		Cadillac	Gas	Hess/Eisenhart Super Rescue Ambulance
1963	$21,000	GMC	Gas	American Fire Apparatus 750 GPM Pumper
1964		GMC	Gas	American Fire Apparatus 750 GPM Pumper
1965		Ford	Gas	Task Unit, Generator, Lighting Plant, Air Compressor, Portable Pump, 200 Gal. Tank
1966		Cadillac	Gas	Hess/Eisenhart Super Rescue Ambulance
1972		Cadillac	Gas	Hess/Eisenhart Super Rescue Ambulance
1973		Dodge	Gas	Raised Room/Extended Length Ambulance
1975		Dodge	Gas	Raised Roof/Extended Length Ambulance
1975	$92,000	Sutphen	Diesel	750 GPM Customer Pumper W/2 Jump Seats
1976		Chevy	Gas	12 Passenger Van, Purchased By Ladies Aux. With Top Value Trading Stamps.

1977		Chevy	Gas	12 Passenger Van, Purchased By Ladies Aux. With Top Value Trading Stamps.
1977	$6000	Chevy	Gas	Four-Door Chiefs Car
1977	$26,000	Horton	Gas	Paramedic Box Unit On A Truck Chassis.
1978	28,000	Horton	Gas	Paramedic Box Unit On A Truck Chassis.
1979	$100,000	Sutphen	Diesel	750 GPM Custom Pumper W/2 Jump Seats
1980		Pierce	Diesel	750 Gal. Stock Line Pumper
1981	$250,000	Sutphen	Diesel	Custom 100 Ft. Aerial Platform Truck
1981	Gift	Willies	Gas	1950s Era Army Jeep Outfitted To Fight Grass Fires, W/Indian Tanks, Brooms, And Shovels.

Bibliography

Primary Sources

Archives of Mack Fire Inc, November 2020
Items from the history of Mack Fire Inc., formerly known as Mack Volunteer Fire Department. Mack Fire Inc Headquarters, Cincinnati Ohio

---MVFD Meeting Minutes, Box 1

---MVFD Photo Archives, Box 2

---MVFD Reports and Papers to and from Green Township Trustees, Box 3

Secondary Sources

"Annual Meeting of Green Township Fire Protective Association Next Monday." *Western Hills Press*. January 10, 1930.

Clarke, SJ. *Cincinnati, the Queen City: 1788-1912*. 2. Vol. 2. Chicago, Illinois: S.J. Clarke Pub. Co., 1912.

"Fire: Destroys a Fine Barn on Contractor Ruebels Farm." *Cincinnati Enquirer*, January 22, 1902.

"First Call for Fire Protection." *Western Hills Press*. December 29, 1929.

"First Call: Fire Protection by Member of Township Association Made Christmas Day." *Western Hills Press*. December 27, 1929.

"Flames: Threatened Bridgetown. Cincinnati Fire Department Called to the Scene--Two Residences." *Cincinnati Enquirer*, September 5, 1908.

Flickinger, Joe. *A Bicentennial History of Green Township: Uncovering a Jewel in the Crown of the Queen City 1809-2009*. Westminster, MD, Maryland: Heritage Books, 2011.

Forgrave, Reid. "Township Anticipates Needs." *Cincinnati Enquirer*, November 6, 2003.

Green Township Webpage. Accessed April 29, 2020. http://www.greentwp.org/.

Hale, Harry J. "Kuliga, The Pretty Land; The Colorful Story of Green Township, Hamilton County Ohio." *Western Hills Press*. 1949.

Hoffman, Steve. "Burned out Firms Rebuilding." *Cincinnati Enquirer*, August 12, 1997.

Hopkins, John. "Blaze Guts 3 West-Side Businesses." *Cincinnati Enquirer*, July 17, 1997.

Houston, Lynda. "Green Township Puts Students on Hot Seat." *Cincinnati Enquirer*, December 5, 1989.

Kiefer, Kathleen J. *Flying Sparks and Hooves*. 28. Vol. 28. 2. Cincinnati, Ohio: Cincinnati Historical Society Bulletin, 1970.

Knepper, George W. *The Official Ohio Lands Book*. Columbus, OH, Ohio: Auditor of State, 2002.

Kramb, Edwin A. *Buckeye Battlefields*. Springboro, OH, Ohio: Valhalla Press, 2006.

"Mack Fire Department Escorts Fellow Firefighter George Zorick III." *Western Hills Press*. June 8, 1977.

"Mack Firemen to Honor Buddy." *Cincinnati Enquirer*, October 1, 1977.

Martin, Rich, Robert Klein, and Roberta Baechle Michel. *We Love Cheviot*. Cheviot, Ohio: Cheviot Historical Society, 2018.

Schaible, Charles. *I Was Interested*. Cincinnati, Ohio: Green Township Historical Association Archive, 1972.

Scully, E. Henry. *Remember When, Monfort Heights*. Cincinnati, Ohio: Monfort Heights Civic Association, 1977.

Silberstein, Iola Hessler. *Cincinnati, Then and Now*. Cincinnati, OH, Ohio: Voters Service Education Fund of the League of Women Voters of the Cincinnati Area, 1982.

US Department of Commerce, NOAA. "The Super Outbreak of April 3-4, 1974." National Weather Service. NOAA's National Weather Service, April 3, 2019. https://www.weather.gov/iln/19740403.

Index

About the Author

Joe Flickinger is a lifelong resident of the Cincinnati area. Joe holds a B.A. in History and an M.Ed in Educational Administration from Xavier University and has also completed an M.A. in History with a concentration in Public History from Southern New Hampshire University. Joe has worked as a history teacher in Cincinnati for over 20 years. He serves as Vice-President of the Green Township Historical Association and also maintains membership in the Coleraine Historical Society and Cheviot Historical Society. Joe maintains professional memberships in the American Historical Association, National Council of History Education, Organization of American Historians, National Council on Public History, and the American Association for State and Local History. Joe's other books include A Bicentennial History of Green Township; Uncovering a Jewel in the Crown of the Queen City,1809-2009, released in 2011; 2018's A History of Colerain Township: From Frontier Wilderness to Suburban Sprawl, and 2021's A History of Bridgetown Cemetery, Quietly Serving Cincinnati's Western Hills for over 150 Years. He is married to his wonderful wife Kathleen and has three beautiful children.

www.ingramcontent.com/pod-product-compliance
Lightning Source LLC
LaVergne TN
LVHW020627100826
845148LV00012B/2075

* 9 7 8 0 7 8 8 4 2 9 8 0 4 *